Praise for

MEDIA MOMS & DIGITAL DADS

and Dr. Yalda T. Uhls

"*Media Moms & Digital Dads* does what every parent who has confronted the 'digital wild west' with their children so badly needs! Yalda T. Uhls seamlessly blends groundbreaking research, engaging storytelling, and practical advice. It is a must-read for every parent who is attempting to navigate a challenging media culture that is here to stay."

—Michael H. Levine PhD, founding director,
Joan Ganz Cooney Center at Sesame Workshop and coauthor,
Tap, Click Read: Growing Readers in a World of Screens

"This book explains how technology has transformed the world of children's education and entertainment, and shows parents that such change is not to be feared! Yalda's deep knowledge of the research and her expertise in child psychology along with her many years as a storyteller in Hollywood make for a unique, important, and engaging perspective. As a parent and a creator of children's content, I appreciate Yalda's guidance and approach; the book is indispensable for the modern age."

—Lisa Henson, chief executive officer of The Jim Henson
Company, executive producer on the Emmy®- nominated
preschool series *Sid the Science Kid*, and *Dinosaur Train*

"What's the best way to parent when it comes to technology? The good news is that someone has finally organized the most current research to help you make the best choices for your family. Yalda T. Uhls combines her experience as a social scientist and an entertainment executive to help make you a better *Media Mom* or *Digital Dad*."

—Cara Natterson, pediatrician and *New York Times*
best-selling author of *The American Girl:
The Care and Keeping of You 1 & 2*

"I'm so grateful for this book! Dr. Uhls offers practical, anxiety-reducing strategies for managing kids' media use. As a mom, she knows only too well that trying to block all access is futile. Instead she helps parents 'fight fun with fun' by making screen time happier and healthier."

—Peggy Orenstein, author of
Cinderella Ate My Daughter

"Educators and parents need unbiased and realistic approaches to the digital world so they can guide the next generation. In *Media Moms & Digital Dads*, Dr. Uhls, a mom herself, gives us a research-based resource, which is also filled with real-life take-aways and actionable steps. I greatly enjoyed this smart and sensible book. A must-read for every parent before they hand their kids a digital device."

—Willow Bay, director of the Annenberg
School of Journalism at the University of Southern
California and senior strategic advisor for the
Huffington Post

"Today, parents living in the digital age often feel as though they have stepped 'through the looking glass'! The digital landscape is an ever-changing and confounding world in which to raise and educate children. Educators and parents alike are struggling with what to do with the numerous opportunities and challenges this digital age offers children in their homes and in their schools. Yalda T. Uhls' new book, based on her extensive research and experience, makes her the perfect travel guide as parents all over the world try to traverse this often bumpy terrain. This is the guidebook you've been waiting for. Safe travels!"

—Reveta Bowers, head of school,
The Center for Early Education

"*Media Moms & Digital Dads* is a well-balanced, scientifically grounded, and thoughtful roadmap of the often bewildering and ever-changing digital world in which our kids are immersed. Parents will find the author's wise advice very helpful. "

—Laurence Steinberg, professor of Psychology, Temple University, and author of *Age of Opportunity: Lessons from the New Science of Adolescence*

"This is a fascinating and deeply practical look at how growing up in this new and amazing digital age is impacting our kids. As the parent of teenagers, I found Dr. Uhls' analysis of how classrooms and teaching have evolved particularly insightful. Each chapter ends with a summary and some reasonable, actionable advice. Yalda's even-handed and open attitude toward all this technology in our lives, recognizing it as a positive tool even while helping us navigate the challenges, will be greatly appreciated by those who work and educate using the tools digital media afford us."

—Kristine Belson, president of Sony Pictures Animation and Oscar-nominated producer on *The Croods*

"Many parents these days are frightened by the media's frequent depictions of 'digital dangers': aggression, sex, and cyberbullying, to name a few. *Media Moms & Digital Dads* corrects many of these myths regarding Internet usage and explains the truth about digital technologies to parents in a clear and comprehensible way, based on facts from research. Dr. Uhls provides reassuring proof that will help many parents overcome their fears about raising well-adjusted kids in the digital age...a "must-read" for parents who care about facts and who raise their children in the digital age."

—Professor David Smahel, Institute of Children, Youth and Family Research Faculty of Social Studies, Masaryk University and coauthor of *Digital Youth: The Role of Media in Development*

"Dr. Yalda T Uhls is leading the way to help bridge the gap between the digital natives (better known as kids) and the non-digital natives (better known as parents)."

—Michelle Kydd-Lee, chief innovation officer for
Creative Artists Agency (CAA), the world's leading
entertainment and sports agency

MEDIA MOMS & DIGITAL DADS

MEDIA MOMS & DIGITAL DADS

A **FACT-NOT-FEAR** APPROACH TO PARENTING IN THE **DIGITAL AGE**

YALDA T. UHLS, PhD

First published by Bibliomotion, Inc.

711 Third Avenue, New York, NY 10017, USA

2 Park Square, Milton Park, Abingdon, Oxon OX14 4RN, UK

Bibliomotion is an imprint of the Taylor & Francis Group, an informa business

ISBN-13: 978-1-62956-084-7 (pbk)

Library of Congress Cataloging-in-Publication Data

Uhls, Yalda T.
   Media moms & digital dads : a fact-not-fear approach to parenting in the digital age / Yalda Uhls.
      pages cm
   Summary: "In Media Moms & Digital Dads, former film executive turned child psychologist Yalda T. Uhls urges parents not to be afraid of the changing state of media but to deal with the realities of how our kids engage with it"— Provided by publisher.
   ISBN 978-1-62956-084-7 (paperback) — ISBN 978-1-62956-085-4 (ebook) — ISBN 978-1-62956-086-1 (enhanced ebook)
   1. Parenting—Social aspects. 2. Social media. 3. Child rearing. I. Title. II. Title: Media moms and digital dads.
   HQ755.8.U35 2015
   306.874—dc23
                       2015021252

For Jim, Chloe, and Walker

CONTENTS

Part Three: Learning

FOREWORD

James P. Steyer
Founder and CEO
Common Sense Media

When I founded Common Sense Media a little more than a decade ago, the world of media and technology was truly a different place. Back then, Facebook, YouTube, and iPhones did not even exist. Our main focus was on providing trustworthy and independent ratings and reviews for movies, television shows, and video games. We had no idea that something called "apps" was an entire category we would need to review. In 2015, we have six categories of media content (movies, television, video games, books, apps, and websites) and nearly 25,000 ratings. What a difference a decade makes.

Our media and technology universe is constantly evolving. Today, kids look at screens 24–7, both at home and at school. Parents are overwhelmed and need guidance. Educators work hard to keep up with the needs of their students. Put simply, we live in a fundamentally new environment, which is affecting our children's social, emotional, physical, and cognitive development in myriad and impactful ways.

Some people believe that media and technology are destroying childhood, while others want kids in diapers to have their own tablets. Unfortunately, many parental assumptions about how media affect their kids are ill informed, with too much misinformation fueling fears. This is why we must look to facts to determine what the true effects are of this generation's 24–7 connections to the digital world. It goes without saying that we need common sense to help us find the way.

I first met my colleague Yalda T. Uhls when she came to work for Common Sense Media in 2011. Her unique skill set—she's a former storyteller and producer turned academic—proved to be a great asset for our team. As Yalda worked to help build our Los Angeles office, she also finished her doctoral work, receiving awards and national press recognition for her important research in the field.

During this time, Yalda became an expert at translating science into useful knowledge and takeaways for parents, organizations, and educators, after using the unique assets and materials of Common Sense Media. It turned out that her many years learning the art of storytelling, along with her expertise in science and research, gave her a realistic and relevant outlook on kids' media. When she told me she was writing this book, one that would delve into the extensive body of social science research at the intersection of media, children, and development, I knew it would be a success.

Yalda's passion to help parents navigate the digital world clearly stems from her experiences as the mom of two children. And as a former movie executive, she is passionate about the potential for media to inspire and engage kids. Yet she believes, as do I, that content creators have a deep responsibility to the children who watch what they create.

Now is the time to answer the essential question of whether childhood is changing for the worse or for the better in our digital world…and if so, how? Parents can and must adapt to help their children thrive in the digital age. As a mother, a research psychologist, and a storyteller, Yalda has a unique background and skill set to help provide many of these answers

Quite simply, *Media Moms & Digital Dads* is an excellent

resource for anyone looking to understand exactly how the digital world affects childhood. It can be essential reading for parents and educators looking for a straightforward book that is balanced in perspective and grounded in facts and research. From analyzing how media affects the brain to determining whether all the likes and "selfies" impact your child's identity development, Yalda gives you a clear picture of interactive technology and digital learning in this remarkable new media age.

Get the facts you need with this book. You will learn a lot, and more importantly...so will your children.

INTRODUCTION

Near the end of the nineteenth century, a new medium was unleashed upon the world. Children took to it like ducks to water, and this terrified adults. Young people everywhere spent hours on end immersed, while simultaneously ignoring the grown-ups in their lives. Understandably, parents were alarmed and worried that this new medium and its racy content were ruining young minds.

When I ask parents to guess what this medium was, they usually presume it was the radio or the telephone. When I tell them it was the mass-market novel, jaws drop in disbelief.[1]

In the late 1800s, parents were worried that the next generation was going to hell in a handbasket, thanks to Jane Austen and other popular novelists such as Susan Warner.* In their minds, the excessive consumption of romantic novels by children was frightening; and because of new technology, which had lowered the costs of print production, dime novels were affordable for nearly every youth. Children shared the racy content and swooned in delight. Parents could not control the rapid dissemination of these popular media.

The substance of the novels was considered risqué, and teenagers, doing what they always do, rebelled by reading as much as they could get away with. The adult population lamented that this new medium was a frivolous time waster, and that youth

---

* Fun fact: Jo in *Little Women* is obsessed with reading Susan Warner's novel *The Wide, Wide World*.

were wasting their lives given the unserious nature of their leisure pursuits.

The novel. Think about that for a minute. Today, most of us worry that our children do *not* read enough books, and we bemoan the fact that nobody reads long form anymore. Jane Austen's works are now considered great literature, and the attitude of that time period is judged as prudish. How could things change so drastically, whereby something once considered unhealthy is now thought to be the antidote to a future generation's maladies?

Turns out, this pattern is not unique, and I am certainly not the first author to point it out. The same scenario happened with radio, film, television, the computer, and, most recently, the Internet. And this is entirely normal. Children, and particularly teenagers, embrace new media; as they develop their identities and separate from adults, they look to contemporary sources for information about the world. In turn, parents panic, not only because we are unfamiliar with the newer technology, but also because we feel shut out and worry about our loss of control over our children's media choices.

Even though we see these kinds of reactions over and over again, in the twenty-first century, people still insist that…this time, it really is different.

And they may not be wrong.

A Unique Time in History

Surveys that measure the time children spend in front of a screen reveal how much the media landscape has changed in the past fifteen years. A trusted source is a nationally representative poll of two thousand children, ages eight to eighteen, completed by the Kaiser Family Foundation. The authors of this survey measured media use over a period of ten years, first in 1999, then in 2004, with the last iteration published in 2010.

By then, children's total time with media had grown to nearly eight hours a day, seven days a week.[2] For the average American child, this is more time than they spend with parents or in school.

Socialization, the process by which people learn to become productive and valuable members of their community and society, occurs through a variety of agents such as parents, peers, teachers, community organizations, religion, and many more. These agents are all, of course, still critical to youth development, but in a world where children's media use has exploded, the scale may have finally tipped.

For the first time in human history, media are the most common means through which children learn social and cultural norms.

Three factors contributed to this extraordinary transformation. First is the cell phone, the most rapidly adopted consumer technology in the history of the world.[3] From 2005 to 2013, the growth in worldwide mobile phone subscriptions outpaced population growth, increasing more quickly than Internet connections.[4] Americans, always enthusiastic consumers, embraced mobile technology and in 2013 reported an average of six Internet-connected devices per household,[5] more than the average number of people in homes.

Second is the rapid growth of social media. In 2004, when Facebook was created, a revolution occurred in the way people interact with screen-based technology. Before then, online communication was limited to e-mail and chatrooms, but post-Facebook, we gained the capability to share, connect, and socialize with a group of "friends" independent of time and space. Today, with more than 1.35 billion profile pages, Facebook could be considered the second largest country in the *world*. All the while, new social channels such as Twitter, Instagram, and Snapchat became popular; by the time this book is published many more will be in demand.

Third, touchscreen technology is so simple that even infants can use it, often with minimal adult supervision. If you haven't seen the video of the baby who thinks a magazine is an iPad, look it up now.* Every parent I know has stories like these. When my kids learned how to crawl, they reached for a stuffed animal, but today a baby stretches toward her parent's iPhone. The data confirms that infants flock to these devices. In just two years, between 2011 and 2013, the use and ownership of mobile technology by children under eight years of age doubled; by 2013, the vast majority of very young kids (78 percent) used mobile phones and tablets.[6]

This sea change is so dizzying that adults think they cannot keep up, and it sometimes feels as though toddlers outpace our capabilities. And even though the pattern of youth and adult adoption is the same as always, the rapid proliferation of these new technologies is unique. The radio took thirty-eight years to reach a market audience of fifty million; television took thirteen years; and Facebook took only two years.[7]

Why I Wrote This Book

During the past decade, I experienced my own transformation. After spending more than fifteen years in the film business working with producers, writers, and directors to develop movies, I stepped off the executive career path to stay at home with my children. Once they began elementary school, I made a decision that radically changed my life, going back to school to get a PhD

---

* "Baby Thinks Magazine Is iPad, " YouTube video, posted by LifeMoments247, June 25, 2012, https://www.youtube.com/watch?v=2vXyx_qG6mQ.

at UCLA in child development. I studied media effects on children, effectively combining my two passions, my kids and media. In 2009, as I began the doctoral program, media use exploded. The timing was perfect: my own kids were immersed in their digital years, and my research on how media affect tweens' social and emotional well-being was informed by the real-life behavior I witnessed. As I read many scientific articles about the effects of media on children, I started to blog and present on the topic to parents, educators, and companies. I found that people were starving for information, along with reassurance, about how to manage their kids' experience of the digital age.

Extensive research on healthy child development can inform our understanding of how this new socialization mechanism affects childhood. As a trained research scientist, I look toward peer-reviewed articles and hard data, which help me parent my own two digitally savvy teenagers. This book, a balanced and practical source that explores commonly held adult concerns, is for parents, educators, and any adult interested in the facts.

Delving into the relevant child psychology research, each chapter of *Media Moms & Digital Dads* examines questions that come up when I present to parents and ends with takeaways applicable to the lives of families. You may be surprised by some of the research, but you can rest assured that the scientists conducting the studies were interested in the truth and the greater social good. As I investigate the social science literature, my goal is to provide the information you need to make the best choice, based on your family values, about how to marry the media world your kids love with your personal parenting style.

My role here is not as a judge; I am a parent, psychologist, and author. I struggle, just like you, to align my world experience and knowledge with the world my children are growing up in. The answer may not always be crystal clear, but I hope the information will be useful.

Media are not going away, and technology will only further facilitate the growth and use of digital tools in our 24–7 globally connected world. We all want to share and communicate—nothing demonstrates this better than the rapid expansion of Facebook—but if we rely only on digital tools to meet these basic human needs, we will disconnect. Realistically, however, kids must learn how to navigate the digital world safely and productively, or risk being left behind. By the time this generation of children reaches employment age, many more careers will be created to meet the demands of the rapid advances in technology. In today's world, for instance, employers look for experts such as "social media strategists" and "big data scientists."[8] This leaves us as parents between a rock and a hard place—we are damned if we do and damned if we don't encourage our kids to explore and use new media.

It's time to do our best to adapt so we can guide children using our considerable knowledge of the world, an advantage we sometimes underestimate. When I give talks I always ask who wants to stick their head in the sand and wish it would all go away. Even today, nearly half the room raises their hands. I hope that after you read this book you will feel prepared and excited about the possibilities. Remember, kids may know media, but we know life.

How to Read This Book

Research in child psychology is extensive, but the application of that research to the study of media effects is relatively new. However, in the last few years, more social scientists, psychologists, neuroscientists, and educators study this enormous and powerful agent of socialization. Whenever relevant, I draw from this literature.

In each chapter, I examine a topic pertaining to media and children and look at the relevant social science research. Each chapter is meant to stand alone so you do not need to read the book chronologically and can pick a chapter specific to your parenting question (however, I do suggest that you read the two social media chapters together). Perhaps you are a new parent and want to understand how to reconcile the American Pediatric Association's recommendations of no screen time for children under the age of two with the reality of trying to keep your child distracted as you are making dinner—turn to chapter 2. Or perhaps your tween is begging for a social media account, and you want to understand the pros and the cons of allowing him to sign up—check out chapters 5 and 6. Conceivably, you are an educator who wants to know what research says about technology in the classroom—chapter 8 is for you. If you are eager to get to the bottom line, within each chapter look for the boxes summarizing the research.

At the end of every chapter, I provide takeaways and a recap of the science. The goal is not only to impart information but to also give a few actionable tools. This is a conversation that will continue, and I hope you will visit our Facebook page, *Media Moms & Digital Dads*, to share how these suggestions worked for you.

Research Basics

Experiment: In this research design, scientists examine a research question by controlling the setting and manipulating only the variable they are interested in testing. Often two groups are compared: one is called the experimental group and the other, which is like the first except for the variable of interest, is called the control group. If a significant effect is found, researchers usually can assume that the variable *caused* the difference between the two groups.

Correlational study: In this research design, researchers examine two or more variables and their association. The variables are correlated if they move together in a pattern, either in the same direction or in opposite directions. In a correlational study, you cannot claim causality.

Correlation does not equal causation. This basic premise is critical to remember when one reads articles based on research. A classic example I learned at school is the finding that when ice cream sales go up, so do murders. These two variables hold a strong positive correlation. Does this mean that ice cream *causes* people to kill other people? Unlikely. People often buy ice cream when it is hot, and this underlying factor (i.e., hot weather) is more likely to contribute to the increase in violence. This example demonstrates that when we assume a relationship based on a correlation, we may ignore other key variables. In addition, without a true experiment, correlation cannot answer the question of cause.

PART ONE

The Basics

CHAPTER 1

Parenting in the Digital Age

Today's American teenagers are the most sensitive, least violent, least bullying, least racist, least homophobic, most globally-minded, most compassionate, most environmentally-conscious, least dogmatic, and overall kindest group of young people this country has ever known.

—Elizabeth Gilbert, American author

Recently, my friend Linda pointed me to a Facebook post by the best-selling author Elizabeth Gilbert (*Eat, Pray, Love*) called "In Defense of Teenagers."[1] She asked if I agreed with the crux of what Gilbert said, encapsulated in the quote above.

Both Linda and I share the joy, and agony, of raising a fifteen-year-old daughter. Living with an adolescent makes it all too easy to judge their generation: the constant texting, the inappropriate social media postings, and the short attention spans. When I was growing up I watched the *Brady Bunch*; the options today include *Gossip Girl* and *Keeping Up with the Kardashians*. Sex and violence in media content seem to increase every year. For instance:

- The extremely violent title *Call of Duty*, rated Not for Kids by the nonprofit Common Sense Media, was the number-one-selling video game title in 2013.[2] In contrast, in the nineties, the top-selling video game was *Tetris*, a tile matching puzzle.[3]

• Advertisements in magazines are more sexual than ever; female body exposure increased more than 50 percent from the mid-eighties to the mid-nineties.[4]

• Between 1992 and 2003, movies rated PG-13 had increasing amounts of violence, sexual content, and profanity.[5]

Perhaps more significantly, children can access adult content more easily than ever. Some details of note:

• Ninety-three percent of boys and 62 percent of girls are exposed to Internet porn in adolescence.[6]
• Grisly news reports are readily available to anyone with an Internet connection. For example, input the word "beheading" into Google videos and 2.75 million choices pop up.

These changes in the media environment represent a sharp contrast from the content those of us who are now parents saw growing up. Given kids' exposure to increasingly mature content, how could they be in better shape than our cohort? In order to accurately answer Linda's question, I took a look at national surveys that track teen attitudes and behavior. Below are some of the key indicators.

Drugs, Cigarettes, and Alcohol

Remarkably, teenagers today are more wholesome than those who grew up in years past. Since 1975, an annual assessment of high school students called *Monitoring the Future* asked a random sampling of twelfth-grade students from across the United States questions about their drug, cigarette, and alcohol use. The study is sponsored by The National Institute on Drug Abuse at the National Institutes of Health, America's medical research agency, and is conducted by professors at the University of Michigan. In other words, you can trust this data.

In 1975, more than one in four high school seniors (i.e., 26 percent) reported that they had consumed an illicit drug (excluding marijuana) in the previous year. By 2013, this number dropped by around 35 percent; the number of seniors who had used any illicit drug in the past year had decreased to fewer than one in five. And this wasn't a one-year anomaly; in fact, in each of the five years between 2009 and 2013, only 17 percent of seniors reported they had used illicit drugs once in the prior twelve months.

Drinking reflects a similar decline, dropping nearly 27 percent in the same time frame. The survey asks students whether they drank any alcohol in the last year. In 1975, 84.8 percent of high school seniors answered affirmatively, and by 2013, 62 percent said the same. Cigarette use is cut almost in half, with 73.6 percent of seniors reporting they had tried smoking in 1975; in 2013, only 38.1 percent of the students had tried smoking a cigarette in their lifetimes (however, it should be noted that recent research is finding a disturbing rise in e-cigarette consumption by teenagers).[7]

Sexual Activity

Today's youth are sometimes called the hook-up generation. So is it true that they are more sexually active? In order to find out, I looked at the *Youth Risk Behavior Survey*, which began tracking a national sample of high school students in 1991; this incredible data set is housed on the website of the nation's Centers for Disease Control (CDC). In 1991, 48.2 percent of tenth grade students had had sexual intercourse; by 2013 the percentage dropped to

41.4 percent. And even though many of us hear horror stories about kids being further sexualized at younger ages (certainly the outfits they wear suggest this), in 1991 twice as many kids (10.2 percent) reported having had sexual intercourse before the age of thirteen than reported the same in 2013 (5.6 percent).[8]

Violence

Given the immediacy and ubiquity of news cycles it frequently feels like the world is becoming more violent. In America, however, crime arrest rates for youth ages ten to twenty-four show a decline from 1995 to 2011; for males the difference was over 50 percent (i.e., from 851 per capita to 423).[9] Hate crime statistics are also dropping: in 1996 the FBI reported 8,759 incidents, but by 2013 the number had dropped to 5,928.[10]

Today's Kids Are All Right

After I ran through all of these annual surveys and statistics, I firmly agree with Elizabeth Gilbert's premise that the current generation looks to be in great shape. Youth today are less inclined to drink, smoke cigarettes, do hard drugs, have sex, or commit a crime than previous generations. In addition, the current society is more tolerant: 55 percent support marriage equality, up twenty-seven percentage points since 1996.[11]. And while pure gender equality is still a pipe dream, we are moving in a positive direction. In a 2012 poll, 97 percent of adults supported a woman working outside the home, even if she did not need to do so for financial reasons; in 1970 only 60 percent approved.[12]

It is natural to worry about our children, especially when they consume popular media content outside our control. However, as you reflect on your parenting rules, remember that the evidence indicates that the majority of our kids are thriving, even amid a sea of change in their media environment.

> **Bottom Line:** Even if children are watching inappropriate content at younger ages, their viewing choices do not appear to affect what they are doing. Remarkably, despite the changes in our media landscape, the behaviors of this cohort of high school students are healthier than ever before.

Digital Immigrants and Digital Natives

Frequently, parents feel overwhelmed by technology. Not only did we grow up in another time, but we also feel like digital foreigners, especially when we compare ourselves to our children. Is it true that children intuitively know how to use new technology just because they grew up with it, while adults are left behind, struggling to learn the new "language"? The terms *digital immigrants* and *digital natives* allude to a difference in the ways that each generation tackles technology. These phrases so easily encapsulate what we all feel that when I bring them up in parent education talks, everyone immediately understands the terminology.

In 2001, Marc Prensky, founder of Games2Train and author of the book *Digital Game-Based Learning*, wrote an essay entitled "Digital Natives, Digital Immigrants."[13] In the article, he argued that technology had fundamentally altered the ways that children learn, and as a result, kids think and process information differently than adults. His suggestion? The educational system must adapt to this generation's new way of learning, and all digital immigrants, aka teachers, must catch up. To underscore his point, Prensky quoted children saying things like:

"www.hungry.com…Every time I go to school I have to power down."

"I went to a highly ranked college where all the professors came from MIT…But all they did was read from their textbooks. I quit."

Prensky's article caught fire because it played into national concerns that our educational system is failing. Many hoped that technology was the answer. Since the article's release, books were written about how to teach digital natives; foundations created grants to fuel digital media and learning; and numerous educational institutions worked to incorporate Prensky's thinking into their pedagogy.

Nevertheless, not everyone was positive and others questioned the evidence. In the years since Prensky published the original paper, research debunked the idea that anyone born in the last twenty-five years automatically uses technology in more advanced ways than those born before them.[14] Nevertheless, I do find that the terms "digital immigrants and natives" are useful jumping-off points to underscore that the Internet can be considered a culture with its own language. Some will adapt quickly, and others will choose not to; diverse engagements with technology are to be expected. Which type of digital citizen will you be?

Demographic Differences in Media Behaviors

I attended UCLA in my twenties (MBA) and again in my forties (PhD); each time, the average age of my classmates was twenty-five. As you might imagine, the experiences were quite different, and the second time around I felt totally out of place. The younger students were steeped in the modern educational system, coming straight from college or research institutions. By contrast, I'd spent the previous years changing diapers, holding hands, and wiping noses.

On the first day of my statistics class, the other students typed away on their computers; their brains seemed to grasp every concept intuitively. I sat frozen, feeling like an imposter in a sea of brilliant scientists. Fortunately, I soon realized that while the younger students had more experience with the software, my knowledge as a former executive and as a mom had value. I was used to working hard, managing multiple streams of information at the same time, and thinking strategically. Within a few months, I had picked up the statistics software program and even mentored a few of the much younger students on how to use it.

These experiences highlight my belief that individual differences underlie many of our media practices. Although adults may be at a disadvantage because we did not spend our formative years using computers and mobile apps, anyone who will put in the effort should be able to pick up the basics.

Internet use and attitudes are complicated even within the same generation. For example, as a mother of two children who are separated in age by just three years, I see a difference in their digital behavior. My daughter, the oldest, prefers paper books; my son will only read on his Kindle. Is this because of when they were born, or are other factors at play? Meanwhile, my seventy-something mother always owns the latest digital device, proudly showcasing her up-to-the-minute technological savvy.

Yes, young children can work a tablet before they can tie their shoelaces, but the idea of a uniformly technically savvy generation has been discredited. Data indicates that adults do not always lag behind the latest generation, even those born after the year 2000, who would presumably be the most digitally savvy. Here are some salient statistics to demonstrate the variety of use cases.

- The average gamer is a thirty-one-year-old woman. Women eighteen and older (36 percent) are a larger proportion of the game-playing population than boys age eighteen and younger (17 percent).[15]
- In a worldwide poll, 59 percent of millennials reported that the Internet was ruining childhood; surprisingly, a much lower percentage of older adults (48 percent) thirty-five years and older agreed with that statement.[16]
- More blacks and Hispanics own smartphones than whites.[17]
- On Facebook, young people ages fifteen to thirty have eleven times more friends than adults over fifty.[18]
- The difference in broadband access between the richest and poorest Americans is nearly 40 percent; 91 percent of households making more than $75,000 have broadband while only 52 percent of the households making $30,000 or less can say the same.[19]

These facts demonstrate the wide disparity in the way people use media. Age, ethnicity, socioeconomics, and gender all come into play. Adults born before 1980 may be digital immigrants, but everyone can become fluent in the language of technology.

> Bottom Line: Media use patterns are a result of myriad individual characteristics and factors—a rigid digital native versus digital immigrant framework does not speak to the complexity of the differences.

Parenting Styles for the Digital Generation

One-size-fits-all parenting is nearly impossible, even with respect to the digital world. To illustrate, in clinical psychologist

Catherine Steiner-Adair's book *The Big Disconnect,* she shares a story about two brothers, with five children among them, who have vastly different parenting styles with respect to media.[20] Each brother's approach was thoughtfully considered.

Dad Eli limited his children's tech time; the only desktop computer in the house had a child safety monitor, the laptop was not connected to the Internet, and the family TV was not set up for cable. In sharp contrast, the other brother, Ivan, had a flat-screen TV, the family played video games, including the ultraviolent *Call of Duty,* and all the kids had their own laptops and cell phones.

Steiner-Adair shares that both Eli and Ivan's kids are creative, thoughtful, and intelligent. Despite the dissimilarity in these family's media environments, these brothers' commitment to being present in their children's lives was their primary concern; seemingly the amount of tech was not the deciding factor in whether the children thrived.

Each family is unique, with beliefs reflected in individual households and daily practices. If you have a television, a computer, and an Internet connection, consider carefully how your media values are communicated through the household environment. However, as Ivan and Eli's families demonstrate, your own connection to your children should impact healthy development more than media rules and regulations.

Media Environments: Families with Children Ages 0 to 8

When my daughter was born, my husband and I were hooked on the HBO series *The Sopranos.* While we watched, our daughter would sleep peacefully in a bassinet next to the couch. One day I noticed her tiny eyes glued to the screen, just as the lead character brutally murdered an adversary. That was the last time we enjoyed our favorite adult content in our kid's presence.

Looking back on this experience, it is easy for me to judge our naivety. Until then, however, our choices were automatically adult-centric, because we had no other experiences to guide us. In addition, my husband and I both have jobs that entail watching movies and TV, so these practices were deeply engrained in our lives. Once our children were born, we quickly realized we needed to adjust. We spent time discussing what was appropriate for our family and set up an environment to reflect this approach.

Studies about households find many kinds of media environments. A Northwestern University study of 2,300 parents of young children, ages birth to eight, identified three models: "media-centric," "media-moderate," and "media-light."[21]

1. More than one-third of the parents (39 percent) were **media-centric**, creating an environment in the home oriented toward screens, usually with background TV playing and a television in the kids' bedrooms, as well as frequent co-viewing of content. Children in these families used screens around five hours a day.

2. **Media-moderate** parents made up nearly half the sample, at 45 percent; these families love media, but other group activities were also an important part of their lives. Their kids spent just under three hours a day with screens.

3. At 16 percent of the sample, **media-light** parents spent less than an hour a day watching TV, and their kids also spent less time with screens (one hour and thirty-five minutes a day).

As you can see, not surprisingly, since role models influence children, the researchers found a strong relationship between the parents' and kids' use of media.

When your children are young, it behooves you to consider carefully the media environment you build into your lives. Start early to set the groundwork for your family's future media habits. Even if you yourself are media-centric, media-moderate, or media-light, you may choose a different style when it comes to your family. Otherwise, embrace your choices knowing your children will likely adopt them.

Parenting Styles for Families with Children Ages 9 to 17

As children get older, they start to use computers in school and own personal mobile phones or tablets. With maturity comes an increasing desire for autonomy. This is frequently when struggles begin and many parents are unsure of the "best" path. A recent survey from the University of Haifa in Israel of 495 parents of older children, ages ten to eighteen, sorted parenting roles into three styles.[22]

1. The first was **active physical supervision**, including installing filtering software, setting limits on time online, and recording a kid's online activity.
2. The second was **active guidance**. Parents spoke to their children about risks, helped them use the Internet, taught safe practices, and assisted (as opposed to restricted) when their child experienced something negative online.
3. The last category was **laissez-faire**; these parents did not interfere with their children's digital lives.

The researchers also investigated whether any of these styles were related to risky online behavior. Counterintuitively, the children who engaged in the *most* risky online conduct were the ones whose parents used monitoring (i.e., active physical supervision).

In other words, the restrictive strategy did not protect children. Other research on filtering software found similar results with teens; these programs were not an effective deterrent.[23] When kids are young, software filters and restrictions can work, but as they become teenagers, this approach may backfire. If a teenager wants to access online content, he will figure out how to work around a filter and may create an alternate profile.

As technology keeps changing at lightning speed, advice about how best to keep kids smart and safe online can be confusing. However, your method can incorporate elements of many strategies. The most important practice is to keep the lines of communication open, allow some independence, and be prepared. Reading this book is a great first step to help you actively guide your children, armed with the facts.

> **Bottom Line:** Many methods and styles exist, with no clear "right" choice. Spending time considering your approach is essential.

Proactive Involvement in Your Child's Media World

Technological advancements, which put us in a culture that's connected 24–7, develop so quickly it's extremely hard for parents to keep up. All too often, our children seem like they are one step ahead of us. I know it feels overwhelming; we want to stick our heads in the sand and wish it would all go away. Even though I am an expert, I cannot keep up with the new apps and games my children use, and honestly, I don't need to. Remember that the basic guidelines of offline behavior apply online as well; the Internet and social media networks represent a larger audience, more permanent and constantly available, but the norms surrounding good behavior and respectful treatment of others should be the same as they are in the physical, face-to-face world.

The statistics in this chapter demonstrate not only that most kids are healthy and thriving, but also that we all use media differently. You can enter your child's digital world if you so choose. In fact, I encourage you to do so. The research in this book can help.

To this point, a 2012 study examined how families with children of different ages dealt with media. Their findings may be useful as you think ahead and contemplate what makes sense for your household and your children.[24]

Families with Preschoolers, Ages 2 to 6

This study found that children of this age group more frequently engage in activities other than media; thus, media consumption was lowest for this group. However, surveyed parents monitored the media choices of their preschoolers less frequently than they did kids in the next age group, school-age children. Moreover, parents were less consistent with applying their media rules (e.g., families who regularly applied rules, such as requiring parental permission before watching a movie, scored higher on consistency with school-age children).

Here is my non-exhaustive list of questions to consider when your children are at this stage.

- Will you allow television, computers, or video consoles in the bedroom?
- Will you co-view with your child? Will the program be age-appropriate?
- If your child watches on her own, how will you help her find the best content?

- How will you make sure that everyone in the family knows the rules and sticks to them (including your significant other if you are co-parenting)?

Families with School-Age Children, Ages 7 to 12

As children enter elementary school, the study found that media use increased considerably and alternative activities decreased slightly. At this stage, parental monitoring increased. Issues to consider include:

- Will television, computers, or video consoles be allowed in the bedroom?
- Will you co-view age-appropriate content with your child?
- How can you begin to teach your child agency in his media choices?
- How will you teach children safe online practices?
- Will you set up an e-mail account for your child? Will you monitor her account?★ When will you allow your children to sign up for a social media account?
- When will you buy them a mobile phone?

Families with Adolescents, Ages 13 to 17

As expected, researchers found that during adolescence kids spend significantly more time with media and less time with alternative activities. Parental monitoring and consistency also decrease

---

★ I put my children's e-mail on my cell phone and found this enormously helpful, as I could track not only their communication with friends, but also with adults. One of the most useful features of tracking their e-mail was that I knew when they signed up for a website or application without my permission and could intervene.

during this life stage. In addition, teens are better able to resist media influences (e.g., copying a character's behavior) than when they were younger. Issues to consider include:

- What are your rules for your teen's social media use?
- Will you monitor your child, and how will you balance this choice with your teen's increasing desire for privacy and autonomy?
- Will you continue to regulate your child's content choices?

As the study described in this section illustrates, many parents begin to more seriously monitor media when their children hit elementary school. I recommend that you start earlier, however, to set up future habits, as such monitoring and consistency in rules should be the norm, even when your children are in preschool.

> **Bottom Line:** Don't feel guilty if your child spends more time with media than you care to admit (or if you do). When anonymously surveyed, most American households report that they do so.

Five Suggested Rules, No Matter the Age

No matter the ages of your children, I recommend five guidelines for everyone, adults and children alike.

1. **Every adult who wants to help children navigate the digital world should consider carefully his own media behavior.** Think about your media use, and what your children see you doing. They watch and learn from us all the time.

2. **Set device-free time.** Find times when the entire family signs off from gadgets and the Internet. This could be at the dinner table, during hikes, while playing sports—it's up to you. It's important for children to see that everyone in the household needs screen-free time, so try to build these into your family's day. Of course it's challenging because many adults use devices for their work, but by making a device-free rule, you demonstrate that family time and face-to-face time are valuable parts of the human experience.

3. **Look toward the positive.** If you don't want your children to tune you out, try not to be negative 100 percent of the time about your children's media choices. For example, try saying three positive things about their media behavior a day. It might make them share more with you.

4. **Live where they live.** If you co-view, you can help children learn how to be critical consumers. Check the ratings; ask them to check the ratings; if you let them watch something you are not 100 percent sure about, watch it with them. You can ask older children to talk to you about the content so you can learn how they process the messages, and then integrate your values into their processing. When they are older, join their social media networks.

5. **Look for teachable moments in the real world.** You can use things that happen in the news to share both positive and negative stories that may resonate for tweens and teens. Bring them up in conversation, not when you are lecturing them about something they did wrong. See chapter 5 for some examples you can use regarding social media.

I am a realist, and I have kids who love media, but I also know I need to help them along. Media are not going anywhere. And kids will continue to use technology to do what they need to do developmentally—define themselves and push boundaries.

Before ending the chapter, I have one more statistic to share: despite the multitudes of devices that seem to disconnect us, 78 percent of respondents in a recent global survey reported having a loving relationship with their families.[25] Phew!

Wrap-Up and Takeaways

Wrap-Up of the Research

1. Statistics that track how much teenagers report drinking, doing drugs, and smoking cigarettes show a steady decline in these behaviors in today's teens when compared with teenagers from the mid 1970s. Violent crimes and sexual activity show similar patterns.
2. Internet and media use vary greatly, and no one factor determines who is technologically savvy and who is not.
3. Surveys find different styles of parenting with respect to media. Parents with younger children range from media-centric to media-light. Parents of older children use a variety of strategies, from supervision to active guidance to absolutely nothing.
4. As children get older, Internet filters are not an effective deterrent to risky online behavior.

Takeaways for Parents

1. Remember that kids are in better shape than we give them credit for.
2. Your offline behavior and media values will shape your household's media environment.

3. It is never too soon to think about your media rules. When you become a parent, consider rules such as when your TV should be on and off, where you will use and charge your mobile devices, and what kind of content is appropriate for your child.

4. Resources exist to help you think through your choices. For example, the nonprofit Common Sense Media, the for-profit Kids-in-Mind, and industry sources such as the MPAA and the ESRB rate content for age appropriateness.

5. As your children become a bit more independent in their choices, consider discussing a family media agreement, which can help you think through what is and is not important for your family. Here are links to a few good ones, and many more are easily found on the web by typing in "Family Media Agreement":

   a. Common Sense Media: https://www.commonsensemedia .org/sites/default/files/uploads/pdfs/fma_all.pdf

   b. Edutopia: http://www.edutopia.org/blog/creating-a-family -media-agreement-matt-levinson

6. When you first give your child a mobile device, a device contract can be useful. Think of it as your own acceptable use contract with your child. Here is a device contract that a mother created for her thirteen-year-old son when she bought him an iPhone: http://www.huffingtonpost.com/janell-burley-hofmann/ iphone-contract-from-your-mom_b_2372493.html.

CHAPTER 2

Screen Time for Babies and Toddlers

In today's world, more and more screens are available to children, and it sometimes feels impossible to keep them out of those tiny hands. Bottom line—most kids will be exposed to screens before the age of two, even though the American Academy of Pediatrics recommends otherwise.

Try this. Go the Amazon site, select the baby department, and input the search term "tablets." Guess how many products come up. 1048.

Mind you, this is in the baby department, primarily for children from birth to twenty-four months, the age at which the American Academy of Pediatrics (AAP) says that children should not be exposed to screen media of any kind. Four hundred fifty-seven of these 1,048 items are actually categorized as baby and toddler toys.

Let's take a closer look at some of these products... There's the Digital iPotty, which has an activity seat for a tablet device, the iPad Newborn to Toddler Apptivity Seat, a bouncy chair with a connected tablet held directly in the baby's line of sight, and the Baby-BeeHaven See 'n Store to keep baby easily entertained with technology while in the stroller.

Marketers everywhere are rushing to promote products that take advantage of frazzled consumers, the low-hanging fruit—moms and dads who want nothing more than to occupy their newborn child. These products effectively take everyday baby and toddler activities, such as riding in a stroller and sitting on a potty, and add a screen to keep the child entertained. And in order to make the sale more palatable, the separately sold content to play on the devices often claims to teach. Babies can learn important skills while they pee and poop!

Decades of research on educational programming such as *Sesame Street* and *The Electric Company* established that television content teaches academic skills to preschool children.[1] But is it true that young babies will also learn from looking at screens? If so, what's the trade-off; what do infants give up when they stare at screens instead of the world around them? When babies do start to use these devices, how can parents bring value to their screen time?

The social science research on how and what infants learn from both the real world and from screen-based media answers these questions.

AAP Recommendations on Media Use by Children

In 2013, the American Academy of Pediatrics (AAP) updated its policy statement to include newer media, and the statement includes some excellent suggestions about how to successfully incorporate media into your family's life. These include co-viewing, monitoring content, and establishing screen-free zones in the family home. The AAP still discourages any screen media exposure for children less than two years of age and suggests limiting screen time to between one and two hours for children older than two.[2]

Learning from Observation: The Real World

I am driving with my daughter, and a car brakes in front of me; my immediate reaction, nearly simultaneous with stepping on the brake, is to throw my arm in front of her body to protect her from jerking forward. It's such a silly thing to do, and my fifteen-year-old makes fun of me. Why do I do this? It's not logical. I grew up in the age of seat belts, and my arm is certainly not an effective safeguard.

The AAA's online driving program states that children start learning to drive at around five years of age, as they watch and learn the driving habits of their parents. Long before I took driver's education, I spent many years in an automobile watching my mother use the arm shield strategy to protect her passengers; she had learned this method when she started to drive because back then cars did not have seat belts. She never instructed me to copy her, but once I started driving I imitated her movement. This example illustrates observational learning, learning that occurs through watching the actions of others.

The Bobo Doll Experiment

It may seem patently obvious that we learn by watching someone or something, but in the mid-twentieth century, many scientists believed this was impossible. Then, in the early sixties, a well-known Stanford psychologist, Albert Bandura, developed a theory that was considered quite radical at the time; he called it the social learning theory.

Bandura's hypothesis was that children learn from watching the social actions of another person, and that neither reward nor punishment was necessary to develop a desired behavior. In order to prove his theory, he conducted a now-famous experiment using a large inflatable, vinyl "Bobo" doll, which had a weighted bottom so it jumped back up after being knocked down. The subjects, children aged three to six, were randomly divided into several groups; half were exposed to aggressive role models and the other half were not.[3]

In the first stage of the experiment, a research assistant led each child into a room and gave him or her colorful stickers to play with. Then, another adult, an actor playing a prescribed role, was escorted into an opposite corner of the room to "play" with his or her own toys, the five-foot-tall Bobo doll, a toy mallet, and a Tinkertoy set. Those performers who were assigned a non-aggressive role played with the Tinkertoys, assembling them quietly and ignoring the doll. In the aggression role, the performers displayed violence toward the Bobo doll. He or she sat on it, punched it, and hit it on the head with the mallet. After ten minutes of "playing," the research assistant returned and led the child out of the room.

After a short break, the kids, regardless of what group they were in, were brought into a room with many toys—a jet fighter plane, a doll carriage, a colorful spinning top. Once the children engaged with these appealing toys, they were abruptly told they could no longer play with them. The children, now frustrated, were led back into the original room and told they could play as they liked with these toys, which now included a tea set and toy guns. Meanwhile, behind a hidden window, the research team took notes. The differences in behavior were unmistakable.

The children who had seen the actor ferociously hitting the Bobo doll replicated the violent actions while the children who observed the non-aggressive adult did nothing of the kind. Bandura and his team asserted that the difference in behavior between the two groups was explained by what the children had observed, how the adult "played" in the room. Before Bandura's experiment, psychologists in the behaviorist camp of psychology (see box) claimed that only rewarding and punishing consequences would affect a child's conduct. The Bobo doll study made clear that other learning mechanisms, in this case social imitation, were possible. This classic study proved what we now take for granted, that what children witness in their environment will influence their behavior.

Behaviorism

In the early to mid-twentieth century, the school of behaviorism, led by scientists such as John Watson, dominated psychological theories of learning. The focus of this field of research was overt behavior (as opposed to inner thoughts and attitudes) because this was considered objective and measurable. Scientists pointed to conditioning experiments, which used positive and negative reinforcements (e.g., Pavlov's dog) as the superior procedure to shape learning. The behaviorists believed that only external reinforcements would influence the development of children, as exemplified in this 1924 quote from *Behaviorism* by John Watson:

> Give me a dozen healthy infants, well-formed, and my own specified world to bring them up in and I'll guarantee to take any one at random and train him to become any type of specialist I might select—doctor, lawyer, artist, merchant-chief and, yes, even beggar-man and thief, regardless of his talents, penchants, tendencies, abilities, vocations, and race of his ancestors.[4]

Mechanisms for Learning: Babies' First Year

More than fifty years after the Bobo doll experiment, we understand a great deal more about observational learning. Thanks to a game-changing technology called an eye tracker, psychologists know that even well before three years of age, children watch and learn from the social models in their environment. Developmental researchers use eye trackers to explore the growth and transformation of the early perceptual, cognitive, and social abilities of babies.

The device tracks the movement of a person's eyes while he watches different stimuli. Through the analysis of the different patterns of eye movements, researchers discovered that a baby's gaze, one of the first ways young children interact with their caregivers, is also a basic mechanism for learning. So, the next time you see an infant seemingly stare into space, watch where he is looking; this initial data gathering is how a baby gathers information, and it forms necessary building blocks for future knowledge.

Perceptual Narrowing on Human Faces

During the first year of life, babies not only absorb and learn from what they look at, they also make critical decisions about what to focus on and, even more importantly, what to ignore. When babies are born, they have one hundred billion brain cells but very few connections between them. As they gaze and stare, their eyes provide information and stimulation about what is important for their development. By the end of their first year, a baby's ability to perceive infrequent visual cues will disappear. In essence, infants narrow in on what they need to know, and forget the rest. Scientists call this change in what we can and cannot perceive a "perceptual narrowing." We see what is in our environment.

A groundbreaking study published in the academic journal

Science showed that young babies were able to distinguish between a series of monkey faces.[5] However, before a baby reaches his first birthday, this ability disappears and never comes back. Remarkably, infants rival Jane Goodall in their understanding of the minute differences in the features of chimpanzees, yet older children and adults are unable to distinguish the same nuances.

Perceptual narrowing explains this phenomenon. Newborns see mainly human faces, as opposed to the faces of other animals. Babies are extraordinarily adaptive learners; why should they waste time studying something like a monkey's face when they will never need this information in the future? Moreover, adult human beings, instrumental for an infant's survival, are crucial to figure out. Once these primary connections are made and solidified, children continue to build on that knowledge.

The *Science* study illustrated how important early visual experience is for developing face-processing skills; "use it or lose it" is literal in this case. The first year of life is thus a sensitive phase of development, as the brain becomes efficient at spending energy on what is critical for effective growth.

Faces are an irreplaceable touch point to early human experience. By the end of their first year of life, babies begin to visibly demonstrate that they understand that a caregiver's actions have meaning. In the next phase of development, babies start to connect the dots. Psychologists who study infant cognition identify two specific mechanisms that demonstrate when a baby is ready to actively take part in the social world: gaze following and joint attention.[6]

Gaze Following and Joint Attention

Imagine you are in a foreign country, and you do not speak the language. How would you signal to a resident there that you understand what she is trying to tell you? You would most likely nod, point to things, or make noises that are common to both languages. But babies don't know how to do these things. So how do you know when they understand you? It turns out that babies provide clear signals when they are ready to learn from another human being.

As your child's first teacher, you will naturally point to many things in her world, expecting her to connect your finger to the object. Watch when your child begins to follow your finger with her gaze; this is an important developmental milestone. Joint attention is similar—a baby's attention can now be directed to an item in her field of vision when she observes another person looking at it. You turn to look at something, and your young toddler will turn her head and follow your gaze to land on the same object.[7]

Once a child pays attention to an object that another person highlights through gaze following and joint attention, her ability to learn through social interaction increases; the visual system is also more fully connected with motor ability, and the fun can begin.

To recap, in the first year of a baby's life, what she sees in her environment will shape her neural networks and form foundational learning. As an infant's brain makes the connection that human faces are critical stimuli, the child becomes ready to engage, interact, and learn from other humans. When a baby begins to meaningfully follow your gaze, or your finger, she can start to share your experience and knowledge.

Bottom Line: What is in a child's surroundings during her first year of life will set the stage for learning from the social world and human interaction.

In the twenty-first century, some of what babies observe, even during their first few years, will be on a screen. Remember the bouncy chair with a place for a tablet? Imagine strapping a newborn into the chair and placing a video of human faces on the screen. Would the baby still pick up that faces are important for survival?

Learning from Observation: The Screen World

Ever travel on a long plane ride with a toddler? My friend Julie, who adopted a one-year-old boy from Korea, experienced an excruciating long plane ride back to Los Angeles. Even though each seat back held a small screen, Jack refused to sit still and watch. When she arrived home, she told her older boy, Patrick, that his job was to teach Jack to watch TV. Patrick dutifully gave it his best effort but was completely unsuccessful. While television sounds and visuals mesmerized Jack for a short period of time, his attention wandered all too quickly. The family was confused: Why wouldn't Jack sit still and enjoy the shows that Patrick tried to watch with him?

If an infant will sit and stare at light and faces, why won't he do the same when he is in front of a screen? We know that gazing in real life becomes learning, and thus serves an important purpose. Can babies learn from watching a screen in the same way that they learn from their physical environment?

Can Babies Less than a Year Old Learn from Videos?

Several years ago, a major controversy surrounding the Baby Einstein franchise erupted between commerce and science. These videos claimed to improve babies' cognitive and language abilities. Sit your child in front of one of these videos, and the baby would mysteriously learn. The company rapidly grew into a multimillion-dollar corporation that hit the jackpot with an acquisition by Disney. But the success brought scrutiny, and eventually a group of researchers published a study that debunked the claims of the marketers. The researchers found that sitting in front of the videos did not teach language to babies. In fact, the children could probably learn just as many words by following their caregiver doing household chores.[8]

Support for these findings comes from several innovative studies.[9] Remember that babies stop differentiating between monkey faces at around ten months; that same pattern also occurs with the auditory system. A famous study published in 2003 found that very young babies could distinguish a variety of phonetic sounds from a foreign language. In a first experiment, the researchers tested nine-month-old American babies and found that they could discern the differences in phonetic sounds spoken in Mandarin.[10] The discovery was exciting; imagine if a recording of someone speaking Chinese or Spanish placed in your baby's room could teach him a second language! Indeed, the creator of Baby Einstein pointed to the research as evidence that listening to videotaped foreign language phrases would help a child learn another language.

However, here is where this study's findings become relevant to the question at hand: the researchers found that these young babies would *only* learn the audio cues from a live human being. In a follow-up experiment, American infants visited the lab twelve times. Each time they heard the same Chinese phrases, spoken by the same person, on either an audiotape, in person, or on videotape. Remarkably, the babies could only hear the contrast in the sounds when they heard the live person. For these tiny children, Memorex did not represent life. Thus, especially during the first year of life, listening to, and gazing at, mom and dad should outdo watching videos any day of the week.

Screen Learning in the Second and Third Year

Adults, watching a baby's eyes seemingly glued to a TV program, often assume that children understand the relationship between screen content and the real world, but research proves otherwise. The experiments on the Baby Einstein products, and many other products prior and subsequent, firmly established that it takes time for children to understand that what is on a flat screen means something about the world they live in. Scientists who study young children and video learning coined a term to note this observable fact. They call it "the video deficit."[11]

In the late 1990s, two scientists launched a series of experiments that investigated when a child begins to understand that content in the two-dimensional world means something about the three-dimensional world. In a first study, they presented a seemingly straightforward situation to both two- and two-and-a-half-year-olds: on a video monitor, the kids watched an adult hide a toy in a room. Afterward, the children were asked to find the toy in the identical room they saw on the screen. The two-year-olds had trouble finding the toy, while the two-and-a-half-year-olds did not.[12]

In order to determine whether the hide-and-seek task was confusing to the younger children or whether another factor was at play, the scientists conducted a follow-up study. Two-year-olds watched the same event, but this time they looked through a window at a real person. Everything else matched the first experiment; the children were still sitting in another room looking at a square-shaped box and watching someone hide a toy. The simple fact that this time they watched the action live helped them easily find the toy, unlike the children who witnessed the identical scene on a video monitor; 100 percent of those who watched the live action performed perfectly.

Surprisingly, in this second experiment, the two-year-olds could find the toy when they watched the action live through a window, even though in the first experiment, when viewing a video of the same activity, they had trouble. The researchers concluded that before the age of two, a child does not seem to transfer what he sees on television to the real world. These findings were replicated over and over.[13] It is now well established that it takes time for toddlers to overcome the video deficit.

Interactive Media: Any Better?

You've probably seen babies get excited about the connection between what happens on a screen and their finger's movements. Scientists are just beginning to test the question of whether interactive media might eliminate the video deficit.

In 2010, this hypothesis was tested with a group of children between the ages of two and a half and three.[14] As in the experiment described above, each child played a hide-and-seek retrieval game; in this case, children witnessed three stuffed animals being hidden by a real person, on a video, or in an interactive computer game. In order to help children overcome the video deficit, the researchers repeated exposure to the content in the video and interactive computer conditions six times. As in the early experiment, in the live condition, children watched through a window while an adult in a playroom hid the stuffed animals. In the interactive computer condition, children observed animated stuffed animals hide themselves in an illustrated playroom; when children were prompted to press a button, the characters popped up from their hiding place. In the video-only condition, the recording was identical to the computer screen condition, but the animated stuffed animals hid and then appeared without any action required from the child.

In all three conditions, after they observed the toys being hidden, children were taken into the real playroom and measured on how quickly they found the same toys. The children in the live and interactive computer conditions were more successful with locating the hidden animals than those who watched the video only. But the children in the live condition still found the toys more quickly.

It also took six repetitions in the computer condition to near the result of just one exposure to a real person hiding the stuffed animals. Even with this advantage for the interactive condition, the real world was superior to a screen-based experience.

As much as it seems that babies understand smartphones from the instant they leave the womb, it turns out that, even with interactive media, the real world outdoes screens for transfer of learning. Why are media, even interactive media, less effective than a baby's actual environment for learning? We just learned that very young children learn through gaze following and joint attention; these means of learning are available primarily when a child is in the physical presence of another human being.

> **Bottom Line:** In their first year, babies need to see faces in person and hear live language, so it is particularly important to maximize human interactions. For kids less than three years of age, from a learning perspective, real life is nearly always more effective than screens. Video time should be limited, in particular when it interferes with a child's natural learning environment.

Nonetheless, mobile devices and flat-screen TVs are a basic element of most people's lives; as such, it is nearly impossible to keep them away from young children. We live in this world, so how do you make the best of it?

Learning from Media and
Real Life Combined

Despite the well-established fact that a video deficit exists, every day more "educational" videos, apps, and games are published. In fact, 72 percent of iTunes's top-selling education apps are designed for preschoolers and elementary school children. And parents truly believe that their children will learn from watching videos. Like Samantha who published the below product review for the *Baby Babble* video on Amazon, we all want the best intellectual development for our children.

Though it's outdated, my daughter (14 months) loves it. It helps me get a break and keeps her engaged in an educational setting. She tries to form her mouth just like they do on the show. She also distinguish [*sic*] between up and down, as well as in and out. We have only been watching it for a month and half maybe. So far still no actual words, but she starting to get it by trying.

One word in this review makes all the difference in whether a child can indeed learn from screen-based media. That word is "we."

In this chapter, I reviewed some of the early ways that children learn, through gaze following and joint attention. Now imagine using these methods with different kinds of media content. Adults can draw their children's attention to important cues on the screen that are relevant to the real world, such as linking a color on the screen to the same color in the room.

In fact, research published in 2014 found that if a parent points to a real-world object that a two-year-old sees on a video, the child can more successfully label the object.[15] This simple action helps young kids interpret the on-screen information and apply it to real life. You most likely label and point when you read books to your child; try to do the same with videos and apps. When parents demonstrate that what is on the screen is socially relevant, children are more likely to attend to the screen. In this manner, children learn that what they are seeing on the 2D screen is representative of the real world.[16]

Remember that social interaction is key. These days, screens also allow real-time communication through features such as video chat. An exciting recent study found that for learning language skills, online communication networks like Skype are equal to in-person interaction; the same study reiterated what was previously established, that video alone is not effective.[17] The key to the language learning in the video chat group was the social responsiveness and real-time conversation. If you can get your toddler to sit still long enough to chat with Grandma online, your child could learn something!

> **Bottom Line:** To help your child get the most from his media experience, co-view and make connections between what he sees on the screen and experiences in life.

Children Under Age 2:
No Screens...Really?

When my daughter was a year and a half old, my favorite time of the evening was cozying up with her in our big armchair to watch a Canadian show called *Caillou*. She is now fifteen, and I see no signs of permanent damage from her early video-watching experience; however, she only watched half an hour a day. Three years later, when my son was born, I was unsuccessful at keeping his television viewing to less than one half-hour a day, because he inadvertently watched the television my daughter watched. Even if he didn't absorb much of the content, he was in the same room. He watched more *SpongeBob SquarePants* than I care to admit, but as with my daughter, I don't believe that these early viewing experiences affected his development. He's a healthy twelve-year-old who is thriving academically.

Most parents with more than one child encounter these kinds of situations. With your first child you can more easily limit video exposure, but once a second child arrives, all bets are off.[18] While my own experience represents a nonscientific sample size of two kids, a recent study with a much larger data set supports my personal observations.

A group of scientists at the Children's Hospital in Boston looked for associations between the amount of television a child viewed—which had been measured over several years (this kind of study is called longitudinal) when the child was six months, one year, and two years old—and language development, which was analyzed at three years of age.[19] Even though the average viewing time for the entire sample of children was 1.2 hours a day, these researchers found no relationship between viewing time and language skills. Significantly, the verbal acuity of kids who watched more TV was neither better nor worse than those who watched less.

Wrap-Up and Takeaways

Wrap-Up of the Research

1. Young children under three years of age learn best from the real world, not from watching a screen.

2. At around ten months, our brains commit to environmental influences, which then form the basis for future knowledge. During this particularly sensitive period, it is vital for children to experience the real world (i.e. language from a caregiver and human faces). A screen may entertain a young baby, but too much time in front of a screen, in particular when the child is immobile, could affect healthy development and critical early learning.

3. It takes children approximately a year before they begin to demonstrate that they can learn from others. Once they reach this milestone, sharing media with a child and making the viewing experience interactive will help toddlers better understand content.

4. Even for children under two years of age, as much as an hour a day of TV watching does not appear to negatively affect their language skills.

Takeaways for Parents

1. It's okay for children under two to have a limited amount of screen time. If you need a few minutes to take a shower, send off that e-mail, or make dinner, please do not feel guilty!

2. Remember, though, that the real world is the stimulation babies need to learn critical skills, particularly in their first year. They will learn more from being outside, from looking at people, and even from a big dog licking their face, than they will from staring at a screen.

3. Balance screen time with plenty of other activities; babies' brains and bodies need exercise and variety. Moderation and balance should be your guide.

4. Find high-quality content and watch with your children, play with them, and make connections between the online and offline world to maximize learning.

5. Take advantage of interactive, socially responsive media features, such as video chat.
6. Finally, watch your own media habits—even very young children are watching and learning, so do your best to set a good example.

CHAPTER 3

The Mobile Era

"Thanks to this video I decided to put down my phone, I locked it away for a day. And it was one of the best days of my life... No one saw it, there are no pictures but the experience wasn't lost, it's all u here and I'll never forget it."

—Swaggy Maggy, May 1, 2015, comment on Gary Turk's "Look Up" video, posted on YouTube April 25, 2014.

On April 25, 2014, a spoken-word poem was posted on You-Tube.[1] The five-minute film consists of a young man speaking to the screen, sharing his thoughts about the life experiences we miss when we stare at our phones. His message was so compelling that forty-nine million people from around the world watched the video. Incredibly, the video, called "Look Up," struck a chord with virtually every generation.

The video speaks to the reality of our lives today, where nearly everyone spends too much time staring at mobile devices. With no trace of irony, the narrator of the video implores viewers to look up from their phones and to notice what is going on around them. The lyrics, available on the YouTube video,* paint a devastatingly lonely portrait of modern humanity. Are they accurate? Are we doomed to bring up kids in a world where people gaze at screens more than real people?

Fortunately, surveys of young people, even teens, find that they prefer to hang out with their friends in real life (IRL) rather than in the digital realm.[2] And although the percentages are close, adolescents still report that they talk more in person (82 percent) than by text with their friends (78 percent).[3] Likewise, most adults claim they use their gadgets to facilitate their family, personal, and work lives, rather than the other way around.

I have confidence that the human drive to be social and to connect in meaningful ways will keep us looking up from our phones more often than not. Nevertheless, the stakes are high, and as parents born before the mobile era, our role is both more important and more challenging than ever.

A Mobile Revolution

The year was 1992. I was driving down a country road in England with my friend Joe, when he pulled out a large, rectangular-shaped gadget and proceeded to call his friend Piper in San Francisco. The two chatted about parties and vacations, and when Joe hung up, he informed me that his family had just invested in something called "cellular technology." He came across as such a show-off that I failed to be impressed by his device. Little did I know that I was an early witness to the transformation of our world.

---

* Gary Turk, "Look Up," YouTube video, posted April 25, 2014, https://www.youtube.com/watch?v=Z7dLU6fk9QY.

The Stats: Growth of Mobile

Mobile phones, the fastest-growing technology in human history, fundamentally changed the way we interact. In 2014, mobile devices and connections numbered 7.4 billion, surpassing the world population of 7 billion people.[4] In 1992, the very first mobile text message was sent.[5] Eighteen years later, in 2010, the world was sending about 193,000 texts per *second* according to Gizmodo.[6]

Mobile phones became more than just telephones with the advent of the smartphone, introduced to the mass market by Apple in 2007. Seven years later, in 2014, smartphones represented 88 percent of the growth in mobile sales.[7] These tiny computers that fit in our pockets allow people to do much more than merely talk and text. Through mobile applications (apps) downloaded onto smartphones, people use their devices for gaming, education, fitness, reading, and so much more. Apps are now a natural part of many people's lives, so much so that in 2013, 102 billion were downloaded, an average of more than fourteen apps per phone.[8] If you can think of something you need, there is probably an app for that!

The growth and adoption of mobile applications and technology show no sign of slowing down. Our mobile devices facilitate our lives, and as people become more dependent on them, it is likely our technology and devices will increasingly enmesh with everything we do and need.

It's a Mobile, Mobile, Mobile, Mobile World

Thanks to the extraordinarily rapid expansion of cellular subscriptions and services, along with the smartphone's capability to perform a multitude of tasks, mobile screens are everywhere. These devices are like an appendage, carried all over—in the great outdoors, in moving vehicles, and certainly in every room in the home, including the bedroom. This change happened so rapidly that, all too frequently, basic human interactions were affected.

Most of us know it is rude to ignore another person while in his presence, yet somehow many people think it is acceptable to take out their phone anytime, even during a face-to-face conversation. Have you ever been annoyed by someone staring at his phone instead of giving you his undivided attention? It is the modern-day equivalent of a person looking past you at a party, searching for someone more important to talk to.

College students report that they have their phones with them when they are in the shower, when they go to church, and even while they have sex.[9] While we become accustomed to the many ways that we facilitate our lives through the capabilities of this amazing invention, we must also make sure that our children understand that, although the benefits are many, there are costs associated with the mobile era.

The Mobile Generation

Children use mobile technology differently than adults do. Babies and toddlers intuitively grasp how to use tablets and phones—swiping, tapping, playing, and viewing. Fortunately, mobile interactive apps and games provide ample opportunities for kids to move their bodies, learn about any topic, create digital masterpieces, and explore everything and anything that captures their imagination. Technology is not *separate* but instead a *part* of children's lives. Digital tools are now an integral part of many kids' daily activities, used in fluid ways to explore their world.

Teens are particularly fond of their devices. One poll found that teens in the United States and United Kingdom would choose their phones over eating out, receiving an allowance, or buying new clothes.[10] Crucially, phones connect teens with their friends, and unlike when we grew up, a kid can easily maintain relationships. Amazingly, in a recent survey of U.K. and U.S. children ages eight to seventeen, 25 percent of the respondents said most of their friends on their favorite social network live a plane ride away.[11] Back when I was a child, all of my friends lived in the neighborhood, accessible by foot or bus, not by planes. Given this early ability to sustain and maintain both strong and weak ties,[12] teens maintain an average Facebook "friend" network that is is eleven times that of adults over fifty.[13]

However, children of this mobile generation must understand that these devices cannot replace many aspects of physical human interaction. If we rely only on screens to engage with other people, we will lose out. Adults, who remember what life was like without Internet access anytime and anywhere, can teach children what life was like in the "olden days." Back then, the chief way to communicate with another person was face to face, and boredom was just a normal part of our everyday existence.

Why We Need to Look Up

In 1995, psychologist Daniel Goleman published the best-selling book *Emotional Intelligence*. His groundbreaking theory posited that emotional intelligence—the ability to perceive, control, and evaluate emotions—is just as important as academic intelligence, if not more so. As more scientists studied emotion understanding, the evidence overwhelmingly supported his early insight. A large body of research finds that people who are more social enjoy fruitful careers, live longer, and are healthier.[14] More recently, neuroscientists have found that our social drives are mapped onto our brain.[15]

Unfortunately, when we look at screens, we are less engaged with our social and emotional environment.[16] Human interaction is critical. Even now, when media are very lifelike and can teach a great deal, they still don't fully represent the rich stimuli in our physical world.

How We Learn Social and Emotional Cues

Have you ever watched the television show *Lie to Me*? Based on the work of a well-known psychologist, Paul Ekman, a deception detection expert (played by the actor Tim Roth) and his team help clients figure out when others are lying to them; they read micro-expressions, defined as "brief facial expressions, lasting only a fraction of a second." These tiny facial movements, which occur when people conceal an emotion, do not involve language. When the characters on the show lie to each other, Roth and his team always spot the bluff. According to Dr. Ekman's website, even nonexperts can be trained to comprehend the meaning behind micro-expressions.[17]

Understanding and reading emotion in social situations underlie the way humans learn, live, and love.[18] We continuously communicate many different cues like these through our facial expressions, body language, and voice tone.[19] In order to successfully interact with others, children must learn to process and comprehend these often sophisticated social signals. Each time a child receives social feedback, she learns to adjust her behavior accordingly. These skills take time to develop; they are not innate.[20]

Emotion understanding begins when babies pay attention to their caregivers' faces.[21] Watching faces and paying attention to the people around them provides children with essential facts for survival: Whom can I trust, who will love me, and who is scary? As babies become toddlers, their skill at seeking socially relevant information helps them make a coherent narrative of the world around them. *That kid cried when I took his toy, and then Mom's face looked angry.* As they get older, kids put various social and emotional cues together to make sense of the whole.[22] For example, a teen can sense when the words people say do not match their facial expressions.

When we communicate through text messaging, likes, or status updates, it is much more difficult to receive these cues.[23] Emoticons, for example, are a poor substitute for tone of voice. Situational context and body language are also largely unavailable through mediated communication. Because children are spending so much time looking at screens rather than people, could they be missing out on opportunities to learn about emotion and the social world? This question inspired a research study I published in 2014.

Five Days at Camp

At a Fourth of July brunch I attend every year, adults and children happily mingle, enjoying one another's company. A few years ago, I noticed a stark contrast in each generation's social behavior. As in the past, the adults were conversing face to face, but this time, the kids were sitting in a row on a couch, facing forward, staring at their phones. Even in the midst of a swirl of activity, five tween girls ignored one another to focus on their devices. Today, this sight is familiar; teenagers socialize with their phones, all the while in the presence of friends. Back in 2010, however, it was disconcerting to see.

I began to wonder whether looking at screens, rather than at people, could shape learning about the social world. Anecdotal evidence abounds that children who stop using media almost magically become kind, respectful, and patient, but hard data is limited.[24] When we don't spend time in other people's physical company, absorbing their facial expressions and the situational context, could we lose out on important features of our environment?

My colleagues and I were interested in whether children's understanding of the kinds of social cues that are missing from most digital communication, nonverbal cues in particular, would change if they were not allowed to stare at screens.[25]

For the experiment, we needed to find two groups of kids who were representative of ordinary children, with one critical difference: one group had to be willing to give up screens for more than a few days. At first this seemed like an impossible task. Fortunately, we found an outdoor education camp, the Pali Institute, which hosts public school children for overnight science and leadership education. The camp director, Jolee Jones, partnered with us to make sure that during the five days the children were at the camp, they had absolutely no access to digital screens of any kind—no TV, phones, or computers. The public school, located in Southern California, was also very cooperative. Two groups of sixth-grade children from the same school signed on to be our guinea pigs: one class attended the camp; the other went to school as usual.

We administered two tests to each set of children, once at the beginning of the five days, and again at the end, and measured the difference in the scores between the two classes. The first test displayed a series of photographs of adult and child faces, forty-eight of them in total, one after another, each held on screen for two seconds. Every face showed one of four emotions—fear, happiness, sadness, or anger. Sometimes the facial expressions were obvious, but other times the emotion was difficult to discern.[26] The kids wrote down their best guess for the feeling portrayed by the face.

In the second assessment, the students watched five videos of actors interacting with one another.[27] The actors did typical kid things such as taking a test or hanging out in the lunchroom. The soundtrack was muffled, so listeners could discern a tone of voice but not hear words. Each participant was asked to describe the characters' emotional reactions, without the benefit of any language cues. In one scene, a girl received a present from an adult. Initially excited, she smiled brightly; when she opened the package, it was an ugly sweater, and she tried to mask her disappointment. The children described the emotions of every character. Later, several research assistants assessed the accuracy of the explanations based on an established codebook.[28]

In just five days without screens, the kids at the camp improved their scores on both tests to a greater extent than those who were at school. The camp counselors told us they were not surprised at our findings. They frequently noticed the differences in their campers after just a few days at the Pali Institute, but our data-driven findings lent credibility to their intuition. Our conclusion was that the time that the children spent interacting in groups, with their peers and counselors, and without devices in their hands or in front of their faces, made an important difference.

When we published our findings in 2014, in a paper entitled "Five Days at Outdoor Education Camp without Screens Improves Preteen Skills with Nonverbal Emotion Cues," the research hit a nerve. The *New York Times*, NPR, and *Time* magazine reported on the study, sometimes more than once.

Optimistically, our results suggest that screen time is unlikely to create irreversible damage to our children's social skills. It took just five days without screens to improve emotion understanding. In addition, many of the campers eagerly embraced their time away from technology. We asked the children to keep a daily diary of their experiences; their entries revealed that once their time was filled with fun and engaging social activities, they barely missed their devices. Here are a few:

Mon: "Yes. I miss watching tv on my phone, going on the computer, playing games on my IPod, and listening to music. I miss my Ipod the most. I think that because I can text off it listen to my music and instagram. I feel weird but i'm ok without it. It's not like I'm dying or anything."

Tue: Missing electronics is hard not to be on or watch but it's okay. All my friends, the councilers, and other people are all so entertaining."

Wed: "Missing electronics is getting easier to be without. Now it's all about me and my friends and I'm not even thinking about electronics"

Thur: "We get electronics tomorrow! Can't wait but being without my phone, ipod, tv, laptop ect. was okay cause being with my friends is better."

And here is another:

Mon: On my first day of camp, It felt different to not be on a computer or in front of a TV. I didn't really miss electronics because I'm not allowed to use them on school nights.

Tue: Today I forgot all about electronics but just friends I felt wierd to not have any electronics. At first I didn't know what to do but the instructors helped me.

Wed: Today all I thought about was camp. I felt happy and different to not be in front of a screen. I feel used to it because I am not worrying about it.

Thur: Today I felt better than my regular self. I had a lot of energy. I have more time without electronics.

While it is tempting to conclude from our study that screens adversely affect social abilities, I believe this is unlikely. A screen is like a page in a book: both can take you away from the social world, yet I doubt many people would blame reading for a child's inability to understand emotional cues. Instead, my takeaway is that, in order for children to best learn social and emotional skills, in-person human interaction is essential. Luckily, most of us enjoy being in the presence of other people. As the first camper's diary entry noted, "being with...friends is better."

When Parents Don't Look Up

Too frequently, we focus on the children who ignore their parents because of technology while disregarding the fact that parents are setting the example. For instance, we have a home video of my daughter as toddler imitating me, matching her voice tone to mine, on her toy phone. If she were a toddler today, I shudder to imagine what the video would reflect; her tiny thumbs would be punching a tiny screen.

Ironically, the convenience and efficiency of using mobile technology means we can spend more physical time with our children, but often we are mentally absent as we focus on our phones and tablets. Research confirms this. A group of pediatricians observed fifty-five caregivers with kids in fast food restaurants; 73 percent of the adults used their devices while sitting at the table.[29] Another study compared the behavior of moms who used their mobile devices while feeding their six-year-old children with moms who did not. During the meal, 23 percent of the mothers pulled out their phones; those parents spoke 20 percent less to their kids and had nearly 40 percent fewer nonverbal interactions. The authors noted that this meant they missed many emotional cues from their children.[30]

These days, you can't go anywhere without seeing a parent with child on a phone. The Tumblr site Parents on Phones hosts hundreds of pictures of moms and dads ignoring their children (parentsonphones.tumblr.com). The captions are sometimes harsh: "My daughter posing next to a mom who has no idea where her kid is." And other times funny: "Holy shit, that's a Dads on Phones trifecta in Fort Greene Park, Brooklyn."

Ever consider what harm could befall a child who trails behind a parent engaged in electronic communication? A study looked at the correlation between accidents on playgrounds and mobile phone ownership.[31] The author noticed that in the seven years from 2005 to 2012, injuries to children under five increased by 10 percent, a total of 137,900 kids. He then examined data detailing the expansion of a cell phone provider in the same area as the reported playground accidents, finding a strong relationship between the two. His conclusion was that parents who stare at smartphones do not supervise their kids, and more young children get hurt.

Physical harm aside, children notice that our attention is divided. *Highlights* magazine's annual "State of the Kid" survey polled more than fifteen hundred boys and girls between the ages of six and twelve.[32] The survey asked the children, "Are your parents ever distracted or focused on other things when you are trying to talk to them? If so, what distracts them?" The children answered that cell phones stole their parents' attention, even more than other siblings and work.

These studies point to the somewhat obvious premise that by looking at your phone you ignore your children. The hard data is convincing and alarming, but if the numbers don't move you, perhaps you'll be swayed by these words from children who told the CNN reporter Kate Snow how they felt about their parents' media use:

"She's always on her blackberry. It's soooo annoying!"
"I hate it when he's talking on his cell. It makes me feel sad."
"I put a timer on the computer. When it goes off, it's time to play with me."[33]

When Is Your Child Ready for a Phone?

I am asked this question often, but truly, the answer is up to individual families. Here are some average ownership facts listed on the website Growing Wireless:[34]

- Children are, on average, twelve years old when they receive their first mobile device.
- More than half of children ages eight to twelve have a cell phone (56 percent).

Many of my friends provide phones to their children when they make the transition from elementary to middle school. I gave my kids phones when they turned twelve.

Mobile phones give us continuous connectivity to the people we love, which sometimes helps us get closer to our kids. As a working mom, I have greater peace of mind knowing that my children have a phone and can reach me easily if plans change. For instance, a bomb scare at my daughter's high school did not send me into a tailspin, because she texted me that she made it out alive. Additionally, I text my children when I am stuck in a meeting and will be late coming home, or when I travel and want to make sure they remember to finish their projects for school. I can also tell them I love them and check in on their day.

Questions to consider before making the leap:

1. Is my child responsible enough for a phone? If she always misplaces her sweatshirts and homework, chances are she will lose her device.
2. Smartphone or cell phone? Smartphones access the Internet, and children will take advantage of this feature. A study by

the University of Basel examined differences in digital media use between teenagers with smartphones and those with conventional mobile phones.[35] The teens with smartphones spent twice as much time on the Internet, an average of two hours per day, compared with one hour.

3. Where will the phone be charged? What kind of plan will you choose?

4. A family media agreement and device contract can help you think through the myriad decisions (a few are listed at the end of this chapter).

To Spy or Not to Spy, That Is the Question

When I was a teenager, I would leave the house, and my parents trusted that I would come home by my curfew. I can't imagine the anxiety they felt, and I am glad I have a tool to help me know my daughter is safe. Nevertheless, using the phone in this manner raises some parenting dilemmas.

I recently asked my daughter how her life would change if she lived in a world without technology and was taken aback by her answer. I fully expected her to proclaim that she would be miserable. Instead, she wondered whether it would be a good thing because I couldn't track or text her when she was out. My husband and I are now thinking through when we should use technology to "spy." This quandary, shared by many parents, is not easy to solve.

A 2009 paper asked 196 parents and high school students to separately answer questions about how they used phones to communicate with each other.[36] They found that children were not as truthful about their whereabouts, or their activities, as their parents believed. Interestingly, when parents called more, teens were less honest and disclosed less information. Conversely, when teens initiated the calls, they were more honest. These findings echo other research on parental monitoring; when teens feel their parents are too intrusive, they perceive mistrust and hide their behavior.[37]

The study concluded with some useful advice. The scientists suggested that, when parents provide their teens with phones, the expectation should be that adolescents use them to inform their parents of their whereabouts. This puts the onus on the child to initiate and communicate. The strategy starts with trust; it's not always easy or practical, but if possible, it's definitely preferable.

Mobile in the Bedroom

In the last ten years, one thing that science made abundantly clear is that sleep is crucial for good health. I used to be embarrassed about sharing my need for at least eight hours of sleep a night. But today, I can point to conclusive evidence that by sleeping more I am consolidating memories and extending my life.[38]

Sleep patterns change a great deal at puberty.[39] Teens' changing sleep cycles keep them up later, which makes it difficult for them to wake up early in the morning. We've all experienced the teenager who sleeps until the middle of the day on the weekend. This is actually what teens' bodies crave: the ability to stay up late and sleep in. Unfortunately, modern society is not equipped to help teens get the sleep they require to optimize their health and well-being. The school day starts early, and as a result most teenagers are living on too little sleep. This has severe health consequences and greatly increases the risk of accidents; for example, 100,000 car crashes a year are caused by drowsiness at the wheel.[40]

So how do media fit into this equation? The National Sleep Foundation found that 89 percent of teens aged fifteen to seventeen had at least one electronic device in their bedrooms.[41] Research is conclusive that children who have televisions in their bedrooms do not sleep as well as those who don't.[42] Yet in today's world, many kids—and adults—have the equivalent of tiny TVs next to their pillows. Mobile phones in the bedroom are used to watch videos, read, play games, or to talk and text back and forth with friends. Any way you cut it, these devices are bound to be disruptive to a necessary sleep cycle.[43]

The facts about phones in the bedroom are ugly, and smartphones are more disruptive than simpler phones. Only 17 percent of teenage smartphone owners switch their devices off or even put them on silent during the night, compared with 47 percent of those with simpler phones.[44] The National Sleep Foundation poll found that the simple act of turning the device off at night corresponds to nearly an hour more of sleep a night, as well as better sleep quality.[45]

Last Word

In the Pixar film *Wall-E,* obese humans spend their days on flying seats with a constant feed of TV and video chat. It's an awful vision for the future, one that is extreme but realizable. As scientific inquiry informs us of how these devices are affecting our children, our culture and social norms will adjust accordingly, hopefully before we fall prey to our worst instincts.

If we build technology breaks into our daily or weekly lives, the gains will likely outweigh the costs. Thankfully, the majority of teens (61 percent) say that their friends understand them better when they talk in person rather than online; in other words, they believe that in-person communication works. Our camp participants loved their time away from media. Even though children's lives are intertwined with mobile technology, they will welcome the break, especially if the adults are joining in.

Wrap-Up and Takeaways

Wrap-Up of the Research

1. Social and emotional understanding (much of it nonverbal) starts to develop before language, and continues to become more sophisticated throughout childhood and into the adolescent years. This understanding is essential for human interaction.
2. The best way to learn emotion understanding is face to face, in the presence of other people. Screen-mediated communication is not as effective.
3. Mobile technology leads some adults to become distracted from child care. This distraction can lead to less supervision, with one study suggesting that an uptick of accidents at playgrounds is related to parents' use of mobile devices. Another study found that moms who looked at their phones while feeding their children communicated less frequently with the child.
4. Sleep is critical for healthy adolescent growth. Children who keep phones in their bedrooms sleep less.

Takeaways for Parents

1. Build device-free time into your entire family's day, even if it's just for ten minutes. Every once in a while, consider longer technology breaks for a few days or even weeks.
2. Help your child learn the importance of in-person communication and teach them the appropriate times to look up from their phones. Model this behavior for them.

3. When you decide to buy your child a mobile gadget (phone, tablet, laptop), consider family media agreements and device contracts. Here are few resources:

- commonsensemedia.org/sites/default/files/uploads/pdfs/fma_all.pdf
- huffingtonpost.com/janell-burley-hofmann/iphone-contract-from-your-mom_b_2372493.html
- promoteprevent.org/family-media-agreements-internet-use-sample-contract
- commonsensemedia.org/sites/default/files/uploads/pdfs/phase3_customizabledevicecontract_design1_interactive.pdf

4. Do your best to keep mobile technology out of your child's bedroom. If possible, charge your own devices in a common area, so that the entire family follows the same practice. Consider starting this practice well before you give your child an Internet-connected device, so the rules are established.

5. If your child has a gadget in his room at night, teach him to turn it off before he goes to sleep.

6. If your child suffers from a sleep disorder or disturbance or from severe daytime tiredness, turn her digital media devices off at least one hour before bedtime and do not allow her to bring devices into her bedroom.

CHAPTER 4

The Digital Brain

The human brain produces in 30 seconds as much data as the Hubble Space Telescope has produced in its lifetime.

—Konrad Kording, neuroscientist

In 2009, scientists at UCLA published a landmark study that looked at how the Internet affects the brain.[1] Cleverly entitled "Your Brain on Google: Patterns of Cerebral Activation during Internet Searching," the research received an enormous amount of press attention. Headlines included:

> Digital Gains Changing Our Brains, Especially Young Ones, *Seattle Times,* April 14, 2010
> The Decade Google Made You Stupid, *The Daily Beast,* December 13, 2009
> Texting May Rewire Young Brains, *The Globe and Mail,* August 17, 2009

Numerous adults pointed to this research as clear evidence that children's brains were being scrambled because of their massive amount of digital time. But the analysis did not measure the brains of children, teenagers, or even college students. Instead, the age range of the participants was from **fifty-five to seventy-six years**, and the study was published in the *American Journal of Geriatric Psychiatry*. These were true digital immigrants; indeed, half of the participants had minimal experience with the Internet!

Nevertheless, the scientists who completed this study were among the first to utilize new advances in neuroscience to consider what happens to people's brains as they search the Internet. After the article was published, the floodgates opened. The feverous public interest fueled writers and scientists to broaden the conversation around this essential question.

The next year, in 2010, the Pulitzer Prize–winning *New York Times* writer Matt Richtel wrote a newspaper series called "Our Brain on Computers." That same year, best-selling author Nicholas Carr wrote a book called *The Shallows: What the Internet Is Doing to Our Brains*. Two years later, in 2012, our nation's most respected scientific organization, the National Academy of Science, put on a fantastic conference that I attended, backed by the Keck Foundation, entitled "The Informed Brain in the Digital World." And in 2015, when you enter the search terms "the brain and the Internet" into Google's search engine, more than thirty-four million URLs, many from credible sources such as the BBC and Livescience, appear.

With this much extensive reporting, one would assume that since the 2009 article "Your Brain on Google: Patterns of Cerebral Activation during Internet Searching," many more studies were conducted to see how our online habits affect our brains, right?

Wrong. Unfortunately very few studies exist.

All the same, at each talk I give, a parent invariably will raise her hand and say, "But what about the enormous amount of the research on how teenage brains are changing because of the Internet?" I wish I could firmly answer this question with reams of data, but unfortunately, there is nearly no research that measures how the average developing brain is affected by its digital environment.[2] How can this be?

The quote at the beginning of this chapter gives an example of the enormous complexity and data-handling capabilities of the human brain. While I am certainly not a brain expert, I do know that the scientific methods used to conduct high-quality neuroscience are costly and time consuming. In addition, recruiting youth for experiments is always a challenge; my colleagues in neuroscience tell me that brain research is no exception.

Despite the lack of research, the question of whether kids' brains are being rewired is a reasonable one. While our brain structure has not evolved much in the last ten thousand years, all life experience affects brain activity. The rapid adoption of the mobile devices that are so integral to adolescent lives dramatically changed the way they socialize, learn, and play.[3] How might typical adolescent brains be affected by environmental influences in their 24–7 digital world? Although the research examining this precise question is in a nascent stage, neuroscientists and experts on digital technology have put forward their point of view.

Expert Opinions: How the Digital World Will Affect Teen Brains

In 2012, the gold-standard survey organization the Pew Research Center, through its Pew Internet and American Life Project, asked 1,021 technology experts to predict the future of the Internet and mobile web's impact on the brains of young people (full disclosure: I was one of the respondents). These predictions presented two contrasting views; one answer anticipated a positive outcome while the other forecasted a dire future. The respondents, a group that included technology enthusiasts, business leaders, and scientists, had to agree with one of the below statements (note: these are shortened):[4]

Number 1: In 2020, the brains of multitasking teens and young adults are "wired" differently from those over age thirty-five and overall it yields helpful results. They do not suffer notable cognitive shortcomings as they multitask and cycle quickly through personal and work-related tasks.

Number 2: In 2020, the brains of multitasking teens and young adults are "wired" differently from those over age thirty-five and overall it yields baleful results. They do not retain information; they spend most of their energy sharing short social messages, being entertained, and being distracted from deep engagement with people and knowledge.

The results were, in fact, mixed. Fifty-five percent agreed with the first statement, and forty-two percent agreed with the second. The title of the report points to its inconclusive summary: *Millennials Will Benefit and Suffer Due to Their Hyperconnected Lives.*

More recently, in 2014, a neuroscientist provided her expert analysis of the literature pertaining to Internet use and the adolescent brain in the journal *Trends in Cognitive Science.* The author concluded the piece by saying, "Successfully navigating this new world is likely to require new skills, which will be reflected in our neural architecture on some level. However there is currently no evidence to suggest that Internet use has or has not had a profound effect on brain development."[5]

These examples are hardly conclusive, but thankfully, they do not forecast doom and gloom. Instead, as the title of the Pew report suggests, costs *and* benefits will most likely arise. Even though brain imaging studies on the effects of the Internet are limited, a consideration of some of the overall literature on brain research, human development, and the intersection of the two can give us an inkling as to the kinds of changes that may occur

Brain Basics

Neurons: Cells that communicate in order to process and transmit information. Neurons communicate through electrical signals and chemical processes.

Synapses: A structure that allows signals between neurons.

Myelin: A substance that coats part of the nerve structure to permit quicker transmission of information in the brain.

Synaptic pruning: The process of eliminating unnecessary synapses.

Hebb's Law: An underlying principle regarding the way experiences affect brain development. Neurons, through repeated communication, form networks (which increase efficiency through myelin) that govern much of our behavior and cognition. Donald Hebb was a scientist known for the saying, *"What fires together, wires together."* The "what" in this case are neurons; "fires" is the communication through the synapses; the "wires" is the formation of the neural networks.

in our children's brains as they adapt to the latest environmental challenge—the digital world.

Recent Discoveries About Learning and the Brain

For most of the history of brain research, the composition of the human brain could be studied only after death. In the last few decades, thanks to new technologies, advances in neuroscience permit a real-time examination of brain responses.[6] One technology that advanced brain science is fMRI, functional magnetic resonance imaging; this is the same kind of imaging that permits a doctor to examine your internal organs. fMRI machines, which measure our brain activity without radiation, allow scientists to investigate how the brain responds to its environment. The research combines the study of mental processes, pictured in brain scans, with what is physically measurable by another human being. For instance, when in the machine, a participant will look at photos of faces and answer related questions. Brain activity is then matched to responses and stimuli to determine patterns. This allows for a more complete understanding of the relationship between our neuroarchitecture and real-world experiences.

While the study of the brain continues to evolve, three exciting discoveries in recent years—mirror neurons, social brains, and plasticity—can help us understand how technology could shape children's brain development.

What Is an fMRI Scanner?

An fMRI is basically an MRI scanner for the brain. This machine monitors the flow of blood to different regions of the brain while research subjects respond to specific stimuli in front of their field of vision. A computer hooked up to the machine then creates a three-dimensional snapshot of the brain. The snapshot shows hot spots of neural activity (i.e., blood flows). Neuropsychologists train for many years in order to interpret these images, so that they can connect the study of the brain with the science of behavior. The research takes a great deal of investment, of both time and money, on the part of everyone involved; thus, sample sizes in fMRI studies are usually limited to small numbers.

Mirror Neurons

Remember the experiment described in chapter 2, in which children imitated the behavior of an aggressive adult who hit a Bobo doll? A significant recent discovery by neuroscientists in Italy uncovered a kind of neuron in the brain theorized to be the underlying means of learning from observing others.[7] They call these types of cells mirror neurons.

The scientists, seeking to elucidate the link between the brain and physical behavior, searched for cells in the brain that show evidence of electricity when animals perform an action. In order to do so, they put an electrode into a monkey's head and tested what happened to the monkey's neurons when it picked up food. They soon found the cell that fired. Unexpectedly they also made another significant discovery.

The same neuron fired when the subject merely observed another monkey eating. In other words, the monkey did not move, but its brain reacted as though it were also eating. Monkey see, monkey *no* do, but monkey's brain behave like monkey do.

They then discovered that exact same neuron fired even when the monkey watched a *human* performing the action. The researchers theorized that this cellular activity partly explains how the brain, even the human brain, learns through observation. Albert Bandura showed that watching led to imitation with his behavioral Bobo doll study in the 1960s; the Italian study connects those findings with the brain.[8]

According to the Italian scientists, mirror neurons comprise approximately 30 percent of our brains.* Think about it—our brains fire and wire 30 percent of the time through simple observation. Initially, we have little control over this function in our brain. As we age, however, we learn to override these responses

---

* I heard this at a lecture by Marco Iacobini at UCLA in 2012.

Brain Basics 2

Reward pathway: A pathway in the brain, called the mesolimbic dopamine system that controls an individual's responses to natural rewards such as food, sex, etc. Activation of the pathway stimulates the individual to want to repeat the rewarding behavior.

Amygdala: An underlying brain structure important for emotional learning, connecting environmental cues (e.g., a snake) with feelings such as fear.

Prefrontal cortex: The top front part of our brain, which manages executive functioning (e.g., self-regulation, attention, etc.) and exerts control over subcortical parts of our brain (e.g., the amygdala).

when exact imitation would be harmful or socially inappropriate. Someone picks his nose, and while our mirror neurons may direct us to copy that behavior, we can stop ourselves through regulatory brain structures such as the prefrontal cortex.

Children develop this skill to override automatic imitation over a period of time. Thus, young kids have less control over their mirror neurons; they fire and wire, and our behaviors are copied.

Our Social Brains

When you think about the brain, do you usually think IQ and academics? Or maybe you connect physical movement to neural activity, as we are accustomed to knowing that we need brain signals to move our fingers and toes. But did you know that our brains also respond and develop with respect to the social world? Indeed, neuroscientists mapped the development of social learning mechanisms to the brain.[9] For example, research shows that the brain reacts to emotional grief, such as an agonizing breakup, in much the same way that it reacts to physical pain.[10] Other research found that the reward system in our brains responds to positive social cues such as experiencing humor or catching a brief glimpse of an attractive member of the opposite sex.[11]

In fact, a large part of the human brain is dedicated to social cognition; this is how we develop the skills to understand and react to one another. Initial evidence came from the anthropologist Robin Dunbar, who theorized that brain size across many species is related to the size of their "meaningful" social group. Humans are estimated to have approximately 150 stable relationships at any point during our life span; this finding has been popularized as "Dunbar's number." Consider this—in a world where online social networks greatly expand the number of people we socialize with, some theorize that the volume of our brains could increase.

Neuroplasticity

An exciting finding about our brains in the last twenty years is that it continues to change throughout our life span. In the past, scientists knew that children's brains exhibited neuroplasticity, but most believed that adults' brains were fixed during adolescence, and were no longer able to develop. Luckily for those of us over thirty years of age, we now know that when you provide stimulation through new experiences and knowledge, older brains will also grow and adapt as a result of environmental influences. The term for this constant adaptation to our environment is *neuroplasticity*.

Remember the study at the opening of this chapter with the fifty-five years and older participants and the Internet? This line of research tested the concept of neuroplasticity by demonstrating how using a computer search engine affected the brains of mature adults.[12] Two groups were measured, a group of twelve people who had limited Internet experience (net-naïve), and another group who had a great deal of knowledge about search engines (net-savvy). While in the fMRI scanner, both groups surfed the web. The researchers reported that the brain activity of the two groups was vastly different; the net-naïve group's brains showed fewer "hot spots."

In a follow-up study, the net-naïve group, trained on how to use search engines, went online every day for an hour over a one-week period. When they returned to the scanners, their brains fired in the same areas as those of the web-savvy group. Amazingly, in just one week, the online environment shaped their brain activity! This is plasticity in action.

The researchers concluded that even when we are over fifty-five years of age, our brains change in response to environmental stimuli. In fact, one of their surprising implications was that the Internet may make us smarter; one of the scientists went on to create brain-training tools using computers to strengthen the memories of older people.

While we now know that our brains adapt to the environment throughout our life span, childhood is a time of particular plasticity.[13] As such, the environmental effects that were seen to shape the brains of the older participants in the UCLA study are more likely to present in the younger generation. In addition, most young people spend 365 days a year online, not a mere two weeks. If this short window of time produced different patterns of brain activity in mature adults, the enormous amount of time digital kids spend with media is likely to introduce similar if not stronger results.

> Bottom Line: Mirror neurons, social brains, and neuroplasticity—the literature on this research indicates that our brains continuously react to changes in our environment. Thus, both adults' and children's brains are affected by the digital world.

Sensitive Periods of Brain Development

The volume of the brain quadruples between birth and adulthood. Much of the changes in our physical brain structures occur during two developmental stages—early in childhood and in the teenage years.[14]

Early Childhood

The first few years of life are a particularly critical time of change and growth. At birth, a newborn's brain is approximately 25 percent the size of an adult's, yet babies have every single one of the one hundred billion neurons of an adult. The difference is that they have relatively few synapses, the structures that allow neurons to send chemical or electrical signals to one another. However, during the first few months of a baby's life, associations between brain cells rapidly accelerate.[15]

While mothers and fathers gaze at their infant, who seems to stare right back, it takes about three to four months for infant cortical activity to present face recognition ability. By this time, the baby makes an estimated three-million-plus eye movements, and each of these movements creates synapses. During early childhood our synaptic connections are more plentiful than at any other time in our lives, with 50 percent more than are present in an adult brain. We overdevelop, and then synaptic pruning reduces our least-used connections.

It takes nearly a year for babies to make complex and accurate eye movements; this is approximately when the social mechanisms of gaze following and joint attention emerge (see chapter 2 for more on this topic). Around this time, infants show patterns of brain specialization for processing faces similar to those of adults. Thus, in their first year of life, infants develop new brain circuits that integrate the visual and motor information in their environment, allowing them to learn from the social world. Seeing actual human faces is how they form the building blocks for future brain development.[16]

Initial environmental influences determine what an infant's brains will focus on. During these early years of brain development, limiting the time that children spend with media is wise.

The Teenage Brain

How many times do you exclaim, "What were you thinking?" to your teenager? To adults, adolescent behavior is unexpected and bewildering; intellectuals and pop-culture enthusiasts alike grapple with understanding the changes that take place during this stage of life. Early in the twentieth century, the psychologist Anna Freud called these years a time of "sturm und drang" (i.e., storm and stress). Later, movies from the fifties, like *Rebel Without a Cause,* and from the eighties, like the John Hughes classic *The Breakfast Club,* portrayed teenage angst and seemingly risky behavior.

Significant changes occur in the adolescent brain. For example, not until their mid-twenties do adolescents fully develop the part of the brain, the prefrontal cortex, that controls executive functioning.[17] Executive functioning is a term that encapsulates the many behaviors that contribute to our ability to control our thoughts and behavior, such as self-regulation, problem solving, and long-term planning and execution, among other regulatory behaviors. These are the kinds of managing functions that parents and educators frequently expect of high school students. However, many teenagers simply do not yet possess the brain capacity to perfectly master this kind of behavior.

In the twenty-first century, findings from neuroscience greatly contributed to our understanding of this developmental stage. For instance, emerging research postulates that puberty may influence teen brain development as much, if not more, than the chronological age of the child. During adolescence, the limbic system, the emotional structure in the brain, exerts power, and emotion reactivity heightens. Studies find that the amygdala, the part of the brain that reacts to facial expressions of emotion, activates more strongly in teenagers than in adults or children.[18] Angry and neutral faces are highly salient for thirteen-and-a-half- to fifteen-and-a-half-year-olds, more so than for other ages.

Adolescents also respond to risk and reward differently than children and adults.[19] Teenage brains show increased sensitivity when anticipating rewards,[20] and this excitement over a potential incentive correlates to more risk taking. Some scientists suggest that the adolescent brain is maximized to adapt to its environment.[21] In order to achieve success as a young adult, a little risk-taking behavior is thus possibly healthy. Without it, your kids might never leave home.

It is no secret that teens care a great deal about what their friends think. In fact, when social or emotional cues are in a teen's environment, the adolescent brain's regulatory functioning seems to be impoverished.[22] Social rejection uniquely activates neural patterns in teenagers.[23] An important finding established that, while in the presence of friends, teenagers take more risks in a driving video game.[24] Their neural processes also reflected this dangerous behavior.

As your teen matures, his prefrontal cortex develops and improves its connection with the limbic system.[25] Throughout the teenage years, the transmission of information between these two parts of the brain increases, which strengthens the connections and allows for improved control of emotional impulses.

However, until then, your adolescent will experience heightened responses to emotion, to peer evaluation, to risk, and to reward, along with lower executive control.[26] These social, emotional, and cognitive dynamics intensify as teens receive mobile phones and join social networks. The still-developing teenager, in this unique phase of brain reorganization, is subject to the same forces online, where friends and digital drama often go hand in hand.

So when teens do things that seem inconceivable to us, online and off, remember that even though they look like adults, that fist-sized structure inside their skulls is in the process of maturing. Teenage brains are not the same as adult brains; as such, applying grown-up standards to their actions is not always effective.[27]

Bottom Line: During adolescence, the human brain undergoes reorganization. This biological change contributes to behaviors such as increased risk taking, sensation seeking, and peer affiliation. Teens will be teens, both online and off. Proceed cautiously and practice patience.

The Brain and the Online Experience

Since the 2009 UCLA study "Your Brain on Google," a few studies looked at how the brains of college students are affected by digital media. One found that the brains of young adults (average age of twenty-three) reacted to positive feedback to their posts on Facebook just as they would to a gain in reputation in the physical world.[28] Another study found that self-disclosure affects neural regions associated with rewards;[29] the implication is that the extensive self-disclosure witnessed on social media affects brain mechanisms.

Jokes about humans developing big thumbs as a result of using touchscreens might have some basis in reality. A study released in 2014 found that smartphone users have an enhanced thumb sensory representation in the brain.[30] Participants' brains were more active in this arena if they used a smartphone versus an old-fashioned cell phone. The cortical activity changed on a daily basis depending on how long the user was on the phone. Thus, the researchers were measuring a small detail of a person's life, the use of a mobile technology, and found that the brain reacted.

A study completed by one of my colleagues at the Children's Digital Media Center @ LA, not yet published in a journal, is one of the few to examine the neural activity of teenagers. The early results, discussed in a video on a YouTube channel called Dissertation Launchpad, found that teenage brains react to the number of likes a photo has on Instagram. The researcher concludes that her findings demonstrate that to teens, social media are similar to the offline social world, in that teens notice and react to who is "popular" and who is not.[31]

Each of these studies demonstrates the iterative connection between real-world behavior, media pursuits, and cortical activity. The online world affects the brain in much the same way that the offline environment does. Indeed, our brains react to every single thing going on around us, which helps us act, learn, and grow.

Thus, as children spend more and more time online, their brains will adapt and adjust. This is neither bad nor good, but a balanced suite of experiences is more crucial than ever. While we use media in different ways, sometimes to read, sometimes to watch, other times to socialize, we also need to balance our use with other activities. Time in nature, movement of our bodies, and in-person human interaction are all important experiences that will develop our neural architecture.

Nevertheless, we are adaptable animals, and our flexibility, which extends to our brains, means that we, unlike many other species, have survived on this planet in many different climates and habitats over hundreds of thousands of years. At the same time, genetics influences brain structure, just as it determines body shape, the color of a person's eyes and hair, and personality traits. Even though our brains and bodies are sensitive to the environment, evolutionary-level modifications will take multiple generations, if not thousands of years, to manifest themselves.

Special Topics: Addiction and Video Games

Brain research takes time and money, and, as in many scientific fields without a clear path to commerce, these are in short supply. While fMRI studies on media use by children and teenagers remain rare, a few do exist, in well-funded areas of scientific inquiry.

Internet Addiction

Addiction to the Internet still is not acknowledged by the clinical community to be a true mental disorder; evidence indicates, however, that screens affect some people in the same way that substances such as drugs and alcohol affect addicts. Brain research confirms decreased brain function in adolescents with Internet addiction disorder (IAD), and the patterns of neuroactivity resemble those of individuals addicted to substances such as heroin and cocaine.[32]

It is important to understand, however, that people with IAD are a small percentage of the population. Many of the studies were conducted in Asian countries where the problem is more serious. Chances are, your kids are fine.

Internet Addiction

If you think you or someone you know might have a problem with the Internet, ask the following questions. If the response is affirmative to more than five of these questions, seek the advice of a mental health professional.[33]

1. Do you often feel preoccupied with the Internet (think about previous online activity or anticipate your next online session)?
2. Do you feel the need to use the Internet for increasing amounts of time in order to achieve satisfaction?
3. Have you repeatedly made unsuccessful efforts to control, cut back, or stop your Internet use?
4. Do you feel restless, moody, depressed, or irritable when you attempt to cut down or stop Internet use?
5. Do you stay online longer than you originally intended?
6. Have you jeopardized or risked the loss of a significant relationship, job, or educational or career opportunity because of the Internet?
7. Have you lied to family members, therapist, or others to conceal the extent of your involvement with the Internet?
8. Do you use the Internet as a way of escaping from problems or of relieving a dysphoric mood (e.g., feelings of helplessness, guilt, anxiety, or depression)?

Video Games

Given the extraordinary societal focus on how violent video games may impact aggressive behavior, it is not surprising that research on how this kind of content impacts the brain found funding.[34] Studies found that players who play first-person shooter games excessively exhibit differences in the processing of negative emotions.[35] They appear to use more of their prefrontal cortex to repress these emotions, suggesting what one would expect: the emotions arise through game play, and players attempt to self-regulate. Other research examined reward mechanisms for video game play and found strong activation during winning and losing. For more research on video games, please take a look at chapter 9.

More Research Needed

Media are unquestionably an essential part of the social life of teens. These days, social learning happens both in person and online. We know that our brains react to the social world, so if teens continue to socialize just as much online as offline, could their ability to learn from the social world be impacted? In a world where the average online social network is well over the "Dunbar number," will our focus on online versus offline face-to-face relationships affect our social cognition? These are research questions ripe for investigation.

Wrap-Up and Takeaways

Wrap-Up of the Research

1. Little research exists on how the online environment affects the average developing brain.
2. The discovery of mirror neurons suggests that unique brain cells react through observation.
3. The brain reacts to the social world. Teens use media to facilitate their social lives and learning, and the brain will be shaped by this activity.
4. Early childhood and the teen years are sensitive periods of neurodevelopment, plasticity, and change.
5. Permanent changes in brain structure are unlikely.[36]

Takeaways for Parents

1. Your brain activity changes as a result of interacting with your environment. Your children's brains also adjust. This is how humans adapt, and it is entirely normal.

2. A variety of experiences, both cognitive and social, is a good idea for balanced brain development. Different stimuli will provide more neural activity and a broader suite of skills. Cognitive experiences could include reading, offline games such as chess, and online games. Social experiences could include community groups, sports, and online networking.

3. Remember the mirror neurons, and model the kind of media behavior you want your children to emulate.

4. Challenge your adult brain by trying new things—maybe even digital media. This exposure can help your brain create connections.

PART TWO

Social Media

CHAPTER 5

Social Media and Social Lives*

I am basically dividing things up. Instagram is mostly for pictures. Twitter is mostly for just saying what you are thinking. Facebook is both of them combined so you have to give a little bit of each. But yes, so Instagram, I posted more pictures on Instagram than on Facebook. Twitter is more natural.

—Female (age sixteen) study respondent,
Pew Research Center, 2013

Spoiler alert! In Jason Reitman's 2014 film *Men, Women, and Children*, adults and teenagers grapple with the challenges of relationships and intimacy in the digital age. As one would expect, the kids in the film snap, text, and post photos of everything in their lives, while parents do their best to keep them safe in both their online and offline environments. Patricia, a high-strung mother played by the actress Jennifer Garner, monitors every moment of her high school daughter's online world, to the point of obsession. Meanwhile, her quiet bookworm daughter Brandy

---

* I recommend you read this chapter with the following chapter. Read together, the two offer a more balanced view of social media. Read individually, this chapter details the benefits and the next describes the costs.

(played by Kaitlyn Dever) bonds with a tall boy named Tim over their shared disdain of the traditional high school cliques. Tim, played by the current teenage heartthrob Ansel Elgort, is a former star football player who quit the team after his parents went through a difficult divorce. Tim and Brandy are arguably the most sympathetic and well-adjusted characters in the movie.

Toward the end of the film, Patricia discovers that despite her best efforts to supervise her daughter's digital life, Brandy created a secret online profile; horrified, Patricia confiscates her mobile phone. Meanwhile, Tim is despondent because his father (played by Dean Norris) cancelled his online video game account, effectively erasing his connection to the online gamers with whom he plays; these virtual peers were Tim's primary social support because his former teammates hate him for walking out on them. Desperate and alone, Tim texts his girlfriend and asks to meet, not aware that her mother is in possession of her phone.

Patricia makes a fateful choice and does not tell Brandy that her boyfriend is trying to reach her. Instead, pretending to be her daughter, she texts back, "Leave me alone, I'm not interested. If you bother me again, I will block you." Cut off from his online friends and girlfriend, Tim attempts suicide.

Teenage lovers separated by the actions of their parents: it is a familiar tragic love story, but with a twenty-first-century twist.

Reviewers claimed that *Men, Women, and Children* painted an unrealistic portrait of how technology affects human relationships. I disagree. While the majority of the storylines featured rare, worst-case scenarios, the depiction of parental confusion and anxiety about how to handle children's digital desires rings true. Certainly, I speak to many parents just like Jennifer Garner's character, who believe that monitoring every moment of their child's online identity is the best way to parent. Other families, ours included, worry about excessive video game play and wonder if disconnecting their children from these ever-present tools is the right course of action.

The adults in *Men, Women, and Children* use their children's access to media as punishment, not quite understanding the devastation it will wreak as their teens grapple with the challenges of their emotional lives. These kinds of parenting choices happen every single day. Taking away mobile phones and Internet access may sometimes be the right parenting choice, but it does not need to be the automatic default. Like the parents featured in the film, we all struggle to understand this enormous force in our children's lives. However, unlike the character played by Jennifer Garner, we can seek to comprehend and even empathize with our children's digital lives.

How the Internet Became Social

Media permit mass communication. When we were growing up, this communication was primarily one way; books, television, and movies are one way, with messages crafted by an author and shared with an audience. The Internet fundamentally changed mass communication. Now, the audience can talk back.

In the early days of the Internet, e-mail ruled. As a young movie executive, I loved the efficiency of this new way of meeting; several people could hold a conversation independent of time and space. E-mail conversations are asynchronous, meaning they're not held in real time. You send your message into cyberspace without knowing when the other person will read and respond. These interactions differ from face-to-face conversations, which require an immediate response. Accordingly, online, behavioral norms are altered. For example, in the offline world, ignoring someone who is speaking to you is considered awkward and inappropriate, but this conduct is perfectly acceptable via e-mail.

As the Internet evolved, people found increasingly swift means to communicate, using technology to socialize in ways that more closely resembled offline conversation. Chat rooms were an early attempt to create real-time contact; users would enter into "rooms" and converse in groups. As with all new media, teenagers were early adopters. However, most chat rooms had no barriers to entry, so anyone could post, and often did so incognito, with only a made-up screen name as an identifier. Adults could easily witness the teen postings, and some became alarmed with what they saw—the inappropriate language, sexuality, and bullying. Chat rooms, resembling online town squares with potential for anonymity, are public, occasionally ugly, and potentially fraught with danger.

Given these concerns, computer programmers came up with new ways to assemble groups, leveraging the advantages of the Internet. And voilà, the birth of social networks transformed our world. Instead of public networks filled with stranger danger, we could now choose who we would communicate with by accepting a "friend" request. And while online behavior itself did not fundamentally change, the closed networks gave people an additional sense of community, a virtual gated neighborhood.

Humans have a natural propensity to be social. Now social media allowed these basic needs to be met. No wonder their growth was exponential.

Share, Share All the Time

I think that people just have this core desire to express who they are. And I think that's always existed.
—Mark Zuckerberg, founder of Facebook, 2011

Mark Zuckerberg was clearly on to something. The rapid rise in the number of Facebook profiles, currently over 1.3 billion, validates his thoughts. Many teenagers today, however, consider Facebook, created in 2004, passé. Ten years later, new social media platforms permeate our digital landscape—Instagram, a popular destination for kids (and not coincidentally bought by Facebook), and Snapchat, a rapidly growing application particularly used by people under twenty-four, and interestingly enough, according to the latest Pew study, used more by more by middle- and upper-class teens.[1] Ever heard of Renren or WeChat? These are top sites in China. Social media are worldwide phenomena.

The growth in these kinds of interactive media, and their exponential adoption by young people, exhibits the primal attraction of these tools. Psychological research can help us understand their enormous appeal, not only to our children, but also to our species.

Need to Belong

When I returned to school in my forties, I was apprehensive. It takes enormous motivation to earn a PhD at any age. Fortunately, even though I was an older student (the average age in my cohort was twenty-five), I found a group with whom I could share my excitement about psychological research and theory. The warmth and encouragement of my fellow lab members, led by my advisor, Dr. Greenfield, inspired me to dedicate hundreds of hours to completing my dissertation; walking across the stage to receive my diploma was one of the most satisfying moments of my life. This accomplishment not only led to three additional letters after my name, it also met a basic psychological need—to belong.

In 1995, the well-known social psychologist Roy F. Baumeister and his colleague Mark R. Leary published an influential paper that provided evidence that the need to belong is a fundamental human motivator.[2] Baumeister and Leary exhaustively reviewed hundreds of research studies, conducted all over the world, to demonstrate that this craving is essential and pervasive. In addition, their hypothesis built on established theories of many other well-known psychologists: John Bowlby's attachment theory, recognized by academics and pediatricians alike, an important indicator of how an infant's connection with a caregiver informs future relationships; and Abraham Maslow's hierarchy of needs, which postulates that humans have basic requirements that build upon each other—love and belongingness come right after food, shelter, and safety.

Here is Baumeister and Leary's description of what satisfies this desire: "First, there is a need for frequent, affectively pleasant interactions with a few other people, and second, these interactions must take place in the context of a temporally stable and enduring framework of affective concern for each other's welfare." Written in 1995, their review predated the mass consumption of online social networks, but the similarity between this basic human need and the features of these networks is clear. One could even argue that Facebook, which has had the same basic design for more than ten years, offers more structural stability than an offline community.

As more scientists studied the appeal of social media, they found that those people who score higher on a measure of needing to belong in fact spend more time on Facebook.[3] Another study found the same relationship with Twitter.[4] While these studies may underscore the obvious, science supports the notion that social networking sites meet a basic human need—to be loved and accepted by a community of friends. It's a fundamental human desire, and it is only natural for our children to long for it also.

Need to Self-Disclose

Why do people feel the need to share so many innocuous details of their lives? Nowhere is this desire to share more obvious than on social media. For instance, how many pictures of food are posted every single day to Instagram and Facebook? I sometimes wonder whether we are a nation of show-offs; if so, social media are ground zero for exhibiting these unattractive human characteristics.

Linguists who study conversation patterns find that 40 to 60 percent of what we say to others is about our own selves.[5] Online, this percentage is higher.[6] One study looked at a random sampling of tweets and bucketed them into eight categories; by and large, the majority of the tweets were placed into the grouping called "Me now," with examples like "Just enjoyed speeding around my lawn on my John Deere. Hehe :)."[7] In fact, Twitter feeds were nearly *twice* as likely to be self-focused as the next most popular category, "Statements and random thoughts."

While it may seem that the people who talk about themselves excessively are narcissists, pathological narcissism affects only a small percentage of the population. Instead, we are wired to love talking about ourselves, and recent brain research confirms that self-disclosure engages our reward system. A study published in the prestigious academic journal *Proceedings of the National Academy of Science* found that we experience more pleasure when disclosing our own opinions and attitudes than when judging those of another person.[8] In this study, each person could choose one of several questions to answer—one permitted participants to self-disclose and share their views, and another offered the opportunity to speculate about what another person was thinking. Each option was tied to a small dollar amount (i.e., $.01–.04 per trial). Depending on which question they chose, participants could maximize their payout (the dollar amount fluctuated between the questions).

Sixty-nine percent of the time the subjects chose the self-focused question, giving up an average of $.63 per trial so they could talk about themselves. Self-disclosing was more desirable than making money! Looks like Dale Carnegie was right: simply listen to someone speak about himself, and you can win in business.

In the last few years, scientists connected online communication to the desire for self-disclosure.[9] We love to share our thoughts and opinions, and the tools of online networking sites make it exceedingly simple to do so. Can we blame our children for giving in to these very basic human desires?

> **Bottom Line:** Social media meet basic human needs.

Research on Social Media and Teens

To adults, social media seem separate from the "real" world. Yet most teens see no division. Today's youth, who grew up with mobile technology ever present in their lives, have seamlessly integrated their online and offline personas. This generation uses theses tools to accomplish normative adolescent drives, connect with friends, and separate from their parents, all processes that are critical to adolescents' healthy growth and identity development.[10] Nevertheless, parents worry about their children's obsessions with online networks and apps. My husband and I included.

My fifteen-year-old daughter tells me that she actively updates at least four social media accounts, mostly through the apps on her mobile phone: Snapchat, Instagram, Facebook, and Twitter. She scrolls through Snapchat, sending updates to friends, usually a sound bite photo or video with a caption. She has many more followers than I do! As a parent, I constantly stress about the enormous amount of time she "wastes" online talking to her friends about topics I deem unimportant.

To help me get inside her head, I recently pulled up my diaries, written when I was in the seventh through ninth grades. Thanks to my old, locked, handwritten journals, I gained some perspective on my daughter's often-unfathomable drives. Over 90 percent of my entries were about boys and friends, with a bit of "I hate my parents" thrown in. After I revisited my past, I reminded myself that my daughter gets good grades, is well liked by her peers and teachers, and is also an athlete. Even though her online conduct seems extreme to me, her offline behavior exemplifies that of a well-adjusted teen.

The likelihood is that when you were young, you also spent most of your time thinking about friends rather than adults. Thanks to mobile technology, typical teenage forces enter warp speed. When our generation went to bed, travelled on vacation with our families, or drove in the car, we were naturally separated from our peers; therefore, we were forced to escape the constant pressure to fit in and socialize.

In the twenty-first century, because teens are able to share, post, and communicate with their friends 24–7 from any place a cellular or Internet connection exists, social demands are ever present. This radical difference between the generations seems alarming, but overwhelmingly, research on social media finds that our kids are adjusting.[11] If a problem behavior is not present at school or in other offline activities, chances are that little is amiss in the digital world.

While it seems like our teens want to hide behind a screen, for the most part, they care about the technology because it connects them to their friends.[12] Interestingly, studies report that those teens who love to be social use digital tools more frequently; for example, kids who use phones in the old-fashioned manner, to speak to someone, are also the kids who text the most. In other words, the majority of teens do not avoid real-person interaction through these devices; quite the contrary—they use them to enhance their relationships.[13]

Humans evolved to communicate in person, and this evolutionary drive will not disappear that easily. In my parent talks, I always share the results of a nationally representative survey by Common Sense Media, in which adolescents said they prefer to communicate face to face, even more than through texting.[14] Other surveys confirm this finding.[15] We are social creatures, after all, and our media now afford that capability.

Preteens: Facts and Stats

Larry, a father at one of my talks, informed the group that when websites ask him for his year of birth, he lists 1904. He does this to avoid advertising; not too many products are being sold to the over-one hundred demographic. Guess what? If Larry figured out how to lie about his age on a website, so can his eleven-year-old daughter. In fact, nearly 40 percent of tweens admit to lying about their age so they can create an online profile. Thus, even though the majority of social media sites do not allow children under thirteen years of age, a motivated child can easily sign up.

Given the legal restrictions on collecting data on children under thirteen, surveys for this age group are limited. However, a few do exist. In a study I led at UCLA on the relationship of the values and media practices of preteens, I collected survey data from 315 children, ages nine to fifteen years, from across the United States.[17] After first approaching parents, we directed our questions to children. Our research question required determining who had online profiles; 22 percent of the children who said yes were under thirteen, and nearly 60 percent of that group were eleven and under. *Consumer Reports* also completed a survey

COPPA (Children's Online Privacy Protection Act)

COPPA is a federal law that authorizes the Federal Trade Commission (FTC) to issue and enforce regulations regarding online collection of information from children.[16] The law states that if a website or mobile app collects data on any child less than thirteen years of age the site must inform and receive "verifiable" parental consent from the child's parent. As a result of COPPA, most social media sites and apps do not allow children less than thirteen years of age to use their services. Some sites are "COPPA compliant," which means they are targeted to younger children and, as such, will inform parents, and get their approval of what data, if any, are collected on their child.

of this age group in 2011.[18] It found that 38 percent of minors on Facebook were less than thirteen years of age. Thus, despite the COPPA regulation, plenty of children and preteens seem to have a presence on social media.

Age 13 and Above: Facts and Stats

Social scientists by and large report that adolescents use media to learn about the social world. No surprise—teens are the most ardent users of social media, with an average network consisting of one hundred and forty-five "friends."[19] As they become more familiar with the content, teens learn sophisticated techniques to manage their online reputation. For example, one of my daughter's friends refused to post a second photo within twenty-four hours because he said that would be "Instagram suicide."

Revising profile photos is an important component of a teen's online image. Teens curate their content, manipulate it to get the maximum number of likes, and remove photos with too few likes. Moreover, teens actively manage their list of "friends" and "followers." In fact, seven out of ten kids report they deleted people from their network.[20]

Research found that teens talk to their friends about the things that concern them the most—school and social lives. Surprisingly, teens go online frequently to discuss school; 77 percent of 10–13 year olds report that schoolwork is an important online activity.[21] While negative postings do occur, nearly two-thirds of teens report that an online experience made them feel better about themselves.

Adolescents also share a great deal of personal information online. Seventy-one percent post their school name and the city where they live; 53 percent post their e-mail address; and 20 percent post their cell phone numbers. Children don't express concern over third-party access to their data—only 9 percent care about this issue, yet one in three say they receive advertisements that are inappropriate for their age. By contrast, 81 percent of parents report that they care about this issue, perhaps because we understand the amount of spam headed our way.[22]

Online = Offline

As they say, a picture is worth a thousand words. In 2012, social scientists from the University of Pennsylvania crunched more than seven hundred million words from Facebook posts of 75,000 volunteers, ages thirteen to sixty-five.[23] Next, they sorted the data by gender and age to create word clouds, a visual representation of frequently used words. The findings are striking, and demonstrate how the online world mirrors the offline world. Here are the word clouds for each gender.

Source: University of Pennsylvania, 2012

In the above, the top cloud with the words "shopping," "excited," and "<3" are from female users, while the bottom cloud with "fuck," "wishes_he," and "xbox" are from male users. The words with the largest-sized font more strongly correlate with the gender. As the above figure demonstrates, gender stereotypes are real, even in the virtual world.

Here is the cloud for different age groups; one can see the reflection of normal human concerns depending on the life stage. In high school and college, we post about school; in our twenties, we write about work; and in our thirties, we share about our children. I don't know about you, but it's reassuring for me to see these patterns online. The more things change, the more they stay the same, even online.

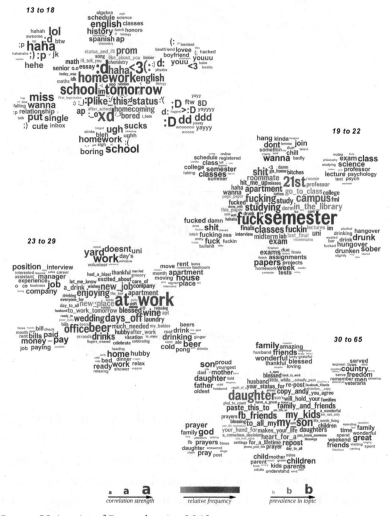

Source: University of Pennsylvania, 2012

New Social Media, New Worries

Parents are continuously surprised by every new app that is created; each one seems to lead to a new way of communication fraught with danger. It is nearly impossible to keep up, and by the time this book is published, the ones I describe will likely mature. However, most applications play in the same sandbox; thus, it's a good idea to understand the overall features. As new apps become popular, chances are the parental concerns will be the same.

Conversational Messaging Apps

Messaging applications allow you to instantly "converse" with someone in your network. Typical features are: (1) one reaches friends in the moment; and (2) it is easy to access the messages on a mobile device. Kids love this way of communicating, as it is instantaneous and fun.

One of the latest messaging apps is Snapchat. While some adults worry that Snapchat allows rampant sexting (i.e., sending virtual sexualized photos), the young men who developed this app did so to create a mediated communication that more closely resembles face-to-face conversation, which happens in real time and disappears with the snap of a finger.[24] Here is the company's young founder, Evan Spiegel, talking in his 2014 AXS Partner Summit keynote about how teens use this application: "That's what Snapchat is all about. Talking through content not around it. With friends, not strangers. Identity tied to now, today. Room for growth, emotional risk, expression, mistakes, room for you."[25]

My daughter uses this app more frequently with her good friends than with acquaintances; it is used in a more authentic and casual manner than Instagram.[26] Other current apps in this vein include Kik and WhatsApp.

Microblogging Sites

Microblogging distinguishes itself from traditional blogging by the length of the posts. Twitter is becoming more popular with teens and 33 percent reporting to use it;[27] users post short messages, 140 characters or less, to their followers. Because celebrities frequently tweet and their handlers know how to court fans, kids follow their favorite stars. Tumblr is another microblogging site where users post visual content.

Photo- and Video-Sharing Apps

Online communication used to be heavily text based. As it became easier to upload photos and videos online and on our phones, the social networking platform Instagram began to rival Facebook as the place for youth to share; the Pew Research Center's 2015 overview of teen social media reports that 52 percent of thirteen- to seventeen-year-olds use Instagram, and 71 percent report using Facebook. It also found that girls dominate visually oriented social media platforms.[28]

On Instagram, you can easily post a picture and be creative with it. User comments and likes are simple to gather, often appearing within a minute of a post. It's a visual way to test identity and determine what confers status. Teens use this platform deliberately; it's a carefully curated reflection of self.[29]

Others include Pinterest, an online bulletin board that allows you to share photos and recipes, almost like a magazine tear scrapbook. Vine is a social media application that allows users to post and watch six-second video clips. While anyone can post, performers use it to build their audiences, usually with short comedic sketches. The content can be inappropriate.

Anonymous Sharing Apps

Applications that allow people to anonymously post questions that can in turn be answered anonymously are among the most challenging social media for youth to navigate. An early problematic application was Formspring; harassment on the site led to media reports connecting the app to high-profile teenage suicides. In 2015, the newest versions of these kinds of apps, Ask.fm, Whisper, and Yik Yak, dominate, yet the landscape moves quickly.[30] Just yesterday, when I spoke with a classroom of high school seniors, I heard about a new anonymous app, whatsgoodly.com, that was sweeping the hallways of Los Angeles schools. The life cycle of these apps are often short, but can be vicious.

Geo-Aware Apps

Geo-Aware apps link geographical location to the users posting. Yik Yak, an anonymous app, has an added piece that allows users' posts to be seen by anyone within a certain radius, like an anonymous bulletin board. In 2014, several high school students in California posted bomb threats on Yik Yak; the schools took these threats seriously and closed down their campuses. Tinder, used by older teens and young adults, is a dating app that uses geolocation technology; the app matches people with potential dates located nearby, and users can let their matches know they find them attractive with a swipe of the finger.

> **Bottom Line:** Trying to keep up with new apps teens use is a losing battle. Learn the basics and then focus on keeping lines of communication open (see the next page for guidance).

Social Media Guidance

For the vast majority of adolescents, use of social media may cause a few hiccups, but as teens mature, and with guidance from responsible adults, they should learn to navigate the online world safely. In fact, social media can be a good forum for practicing real-world skills such as learning to form groups, getting along with other people, and networking.[31]

In 2013, the Pew Research Center found that only 4 percent of teens reported posting something that caused a problem in their lives, while another 4 percent posted something that got them in trouble at school.[32] Just as we did back in our day, kids will make mistakes, but today those missteps can be documented and come back to bite them. It is prudent to guide your children when you allow them to join a social network. Following are some social media essentials for parents of tweens and teens.

Online Friend Means Offline Parenting

When my daughter turned twelve, she became more insistent about joining Facebook. "Everyone else is on it," she exclaimed. While I knew that she exaggerated, I also knew that some of her friends were indeed members.

Ironically, I turned to Facebook to ask other parents whether they allowed their children to join before the age of thirteen. Many parents posted, "Just say no!," often the knee-jerk reaction of well-meaning parents who want to protect their children.[33] But research suggests that this kind of approach can backfire; peer pressure will kick in and your child may choose to go along with the pack. If my daughter had created a page that I did not know about, I would not be able to quietly monitor her behavior. We ended up yielding a few months shy of her thirteenth birthday.

The goodwill created from slightly bending our rule paid off. She agreed to our terms. The number-one rule? To friend me. Being an online "friend" means being an active parent. We can help our children thrive in this environment by getting involved, particularly as they begin to log on more and more. You may not know the latest app, but you can still parent your kids online.

Think about it—when your child learned how to walk, you stood near her, making sure she did not fall. When she started to cross the street on her own two feet, you held her hand. Eventually, you trusted a crossing guard to guide her, and finally you trusted your child to cross alone, and hoped she would look both ways. Similarly, as your child begins to actively navigate the digital world, you should be by her side, at least in the beginning.

Start by creating your own profile on any network your children join, then send them a friendship request. But your job should not stop there. It is important to periodically check their activity. Check it once a day for a few months and then cut back if you do not see anything troubling. Look for behavior or photos that are inappropriate. Teens are focused on sharing what their friends might like, and they forget that adults are online too. In fact, very few children are able to accurately guess how many people see their posts—they consistently estimate their audience at only 27 percent of its actual size.

The security company McAfee found that 46 percent of ten- to twenty-three-year-olds said they would change their online behavior if they knew that their parents were paying attention.[34] Another study found that 25 percent of teens adjusted their privacy settings after "friending" their parents. Other research examined the relationship between parent–child social networking, connection, and outcomes for adolescents. Social networking with parents was associated with increased connection between parents and adolescents and more positive offline behavior. Conversely, adolescent social networking use *without* parents was associated with negative outcomes.[35]

Once you follow your child, please respect his privacy. If you see posts that are inappropriate, do not post your disapproval on his feed. Ask him about it offline; help him understand that others will judge. These kinds of conversations provide important guidance to your child as he begins to understand that online everyone is watching.

Digital Footprints

When my daughter worked on an ancestry project for school, she asked me to find pictures of our parents and grandparents, so I dutifully dug out my husband's and my old photo albums. By the time I triumphantly returned with the faded photos, she no longer needed my help. She'd found everything she needed online with a few clicks, including photos of several deceased grandparents. Crazy how simple it was; I definitely felt like a digital dinosaur.

By now, we should all know that virtually everything is online, permanent and subject to public dissemination. While I would like to believe that most of us are conscious of the digital trail we leave behind, the reality is that anyone can make a mistake. Even the sexist fraternity e-mails of Snapchat founder Evan Spiegel were recently released, much to his chagrin. Thinking about your digital footprint is an important lesson at any age, but it's particularly important for our children, whose online identity is shaped from a very young age, when proud parents post pictures and videos featuring their offspring.

Employers and admissions officers increasingly use these digital footprints to determine whether a candidate is the right fit. As we well know, children do not have the life experience, or the brain development, to think ahead to college or future employment. When they post, they focus primarily on their peer group.

Thus, it is incumbent upon parents and educators to help open a kid's eyes to the bigger picture. Here are some facts you can offer to bolster your case.

- In 2014, Kaplan found that 31 percent of college admissions officers said they had visited an applicant's Facebook or other personal social media page to learn more about them—with each year Kaplan has done the survey, the number has increased dramatically.[36]
- More crucially for those trying to get into college, 30 percent of the admissions officers said they had discovered information online that had negatively affected an applicant's prospects.

Employers also examine online footprints.

- One study found that a profile emphasizing family values and professionalism increased a candidate's chances of getting a job; conversely, posting photos of drinking alcohol or taking drugs hurt a candidate.
- The online job search website CareerBuilder found that 51 percent of the content that hiring managers found online caused them to reject a job candidate. The most common reasons were provocative or inappropriate photos or information posted on a candidate's profile.[37]

Irreparable Mistakes = Teachable Moments

The news provides plenty of opportunities to talk to your child about his digital footprint, and these teachable moments are priceless. By talking about the stupid things other people did online, along with the consequences, you are educating your child about the risks, but it won't feel like lecturing. These moments serve as a reminder that every word and image posted on the Internet is subject to being copied, pasted, and shared, sometimes with serious consequences.

The following stories were helpful for me to share with my kids (links to the stories are in the endnotes). Remember that these are extreme examples; it is unlikely your child will be in this situation.

- A college student posted a rant on YouTube about Asians talking in the school library.[38] The video went viral and led to death threats.
- When a girl sent a Snapchat of her mom and fourteen-year-old sister getting out of a hot tub topless, the photo was saved and went viral. The local police arrested the mom for endangering a minor.[39]
- An adult PR executive tweeted that she was going to Africa and hoped she wouldn't get AIDS. Then she said, "Just kidding, I'm white." She lost her job and is still recovering from the experience.[40]
- While on a college tour, a senior tweeted disparaging remarks about other potential applicants. Not only did everyone find out, she didn't get accepted to the school.[41]
- High school football players took photos showing their sexual violation of a drunken girl. This evidence, along with the many text messages they sent, was used in court to send them to jail.[42]
- A teenage girl in my daughter's high school posted a doctored bikini selfie of herself fifteen pounds lighter than her actual weight. Another student found the original photo and created a social media account with the two photos side by side. The account went viral in the high school and the girl was devastated.

Wrap-Up and Takeaways

Wrap-Up of the Research

1. Humans have basic needs such as belonging and sharing information about themselves.
2. These needs are met by social media.
3. Teens use social media for typical developmental tasks—identity development and socializing with peers.

Takeaways for Parents

1. Social media used wisely are not dangerous, and could develop useful workforce skills such as networking.
2. Most social media sites have age requirements (typically 13 years and older) in their terms of service.
3. Parents should set ground rules, media contracts can help you think through the rules.
4. Once your child joins, he should friend you.
5. Monitor your child's online posts, at least until you see she is being smart and safe.
6. If you see anything inappropriate, speak to your kid, but do it offline and in private.
7. Talk to your child about her digital footprint and why it is important.
8. Use the mistakes of others, often reported in the press, as teachable moments.
9. Watch what you post, especially when children are young; remember that someday they will be online and will see that "cute" baby photo but as adolescents, that photo could mortify them.

CHAPTER 6

Fame, FOMO, and Selfies*

Think about what people are doing on Facebook today. They're keeping up with their friends and family, but they're also building an image and identity for themselves, which in a sense is their brand. They're connecting with the audience that they want to connect to.

—Mark Zuckerberg, 2009

Alex was just a regular teenage boy. Girls at his school thought he was really cute, but other than that, his life was pretty ordinary. He went to high school, got grounded by his parents, and worked a day job. Then one day, he became famous. For bagging groceries at Target (more about Alex's rise to fame later).

Welcome to 2015, when tweens and teens can use the tools of social media to gain renown. Thanks to marketing stunts, even animals have dedicated fans; Lou's Pet Shop in Grosse Pointe, Michigan, reports that its seventeen-year-old turtle, Frankie, who has a webcam strapped to his back, receives at least ten thousand

---

* I recommend reading this chapter with the previous chapter. Read together, the two offer a more balanced view of social media. Read individually, this chapter details some of the costs and the previous chapter describes benefits.

views a month. Wacha Cohen, the dog owned by the TV celebrity Andy Cohen, has a Twitter feed with 11,500 followers. It seems that every creature with a pulse wants in on the action.

A legitimate career path exists for the most successful; if you build a large enough audience, you can collect ad revenue, create an online video channel, and may even be courted by traditional media companies. Social media offer a multitude of tools that permit a person to demonstrate how admired she is. Teenagers know this, and they ardently court their own followers, likes, and comments. Recognition is visible, public, and measurable. Young people, already focused on friends and popularity, eagerly use these tools to showcase their lives, and in the process, many hope for fame and fortune.

Our teens are immersed in this world of constant attention, and many enthusiastically embrace the ability to be noticed by everyone. Adolescents can connect with their audience on a non-stop basis, with no escape even behind the closed doors of their brick-and-mortar homes. Could the focus on viewers outside of one's immediate face-to-face community adversely affect a developing identity? While most teenagers will survive and thrive using social media, others may suffer under the ever-present social pressures, overwhelmed by the exposure and judgment that previous generations were able to leave behind at school. Hard data is scarce, but social science can inform the debate.

Psychological Mechanisms Meet Social Media Features

Psychologists have studied impression management and social comparison for decades; these common human activities are accelerated in a world where we compare ourselves not only to our neighbors but also to the world at large on a continuous basis.

Impression Management and Performance

Most of us manage the way we appear to other people by doing our best to look good and act in a positive manner. Impression management is the psychological term for attempting to control your appearance to others. Here is the definition: "Impression management (also called self-presentation) refers to the process by which individuals attempt to control the impressions others form of them."[1]

Celebrities, many of whom have teams that help them portray a carefully crafted image, are masters at this practice. Meanwhile, the rest of us muddle along, trying our best to appear fabulous.

In 1956, the sociologist Erving Goffman wrote an influential book called *The Presentation of Self in Everyday Life.*[2] In it he deconstructed the myriad techniques humans use when presenting themselves to others in face-to-face communication. He theorized that when we interact with another person or with a group, we "perform." It's an apt description for behavior online, where one performs for an invisible audience that is continuously present and critiquing.

Undoubtedly, online social networks map on to these theoretical constructs. Moreover, social media allow people to craft their image without the required pressure of an immediate response. Online, you can actively manage your impression for maximum impact. Accordingly, as we "dress up" and show off our most attractive features, it's always a first date on social media. However, if you spend too much time "performing," you risk not "being." Not only by losing out on being present in your life, but also by creating an image out of sync with reality.

Social Comparison

"Keeping up with the Joneses" has long been a concern, demonstrated by a comic strip of that name that debuted in 1913, and which featured unseen neighbors, the Joneses, whose lifestyle the neighbors never could quite match. The American social psychologist Leon Festinger, famous for cognitive dissonance theory, developed another powerful premise, the social comparison theory, to explain this fundamental human practice. Dr. Festinger conjectured that we compare ourselves with others in order to better understand our own attitudes and actions. When you attempt self-evaluation, you limit your perspective to your internal thoughts, which are both incomplete and subjective. External benchmarks guide us on what is socially "acceptable." We look to other people, we contrast ourselves, and then we change our behavior to fit in or keep up.

As with impression management, too much social comparison can lead to inauthentic behavior. When we compare "upward," we look to people more accomplished or more desirable than ourselves. Upward comparison at its best can motivate a self-improvement kick, but at other times it can produce a feeling of inadequacy. For example, the fashion and diet industries thrive because of this fundamental human characteristic; only 2 percent of American women are model thin,[3] yet all too many of us all strive to reach this impossible standard.

Online networks hold all the factors for social comparison. Hundreds of thousands of online photos and status updates are data points that encourage us to try keeping up with the Joneses on a nonstop basis.[4] In addition, because most people manage their impressions online, posts are overwhelmingly positive, and thus the opportunities for upward comparisons abound. Photoshop and apps like Perfect365 allow everyone to post an ideal, yet fake, selfie. Mature social network users will hopefully have a secure self-image, as well as a healthy skepticism regarding the authentic nature of others' posts. However, many young people lack this understanding.

> **Bottom Line:** Well-studied psychological mechanisms are in full force on social networks. Adults have experience with these; kids are learning. Help your child with your adult eyes, brain, and knowledge.

Tweens and Teens: A Perfect Storm

In the tween years, social comparison and impression management are in high gear, as friends become the barometers of all things. Teenagers, hoping for popularity, use online tools to curate their image and search for status through attempts to gather large numbers of followers, likes, and comments. These visible and public markers demonstrate to their friends their place in the social order.

In addition, children often receive their first mobile phone as tweens or young teens, and their ability to interact with peers is then instant and ever present. Other changes in a preadolescent's understanding of the social world also emerge during this time period—kids become more aware that material goods confer prestige,[5] and they learn to make more sophisticated social comparisons.[6]

Try thinking about some of your most memorable experiences, both painful and exciting; they may be from your teenage years. Psychologists now believe that teenagers are particularly sensitive to their social environment, even more so than children and adults.[7] Several psychological constructs, particularly important during adolescence, are relevant to explore. As teens form identities, search for popularity, and look to peers, their online environment, frequently social, is bound to shape their development.

Identity Development

Until my daughter became a teenager, I did not quite understand the meaning of identity formation. I suspected it was an academic concept created to overly complicate typical human behavior. But one day, the classroom theory connected to my own life. My daughter informed me that she was one of the few girls in her school group who cared about her grades. As she shared her confusion, I understood her search to find personal meaning in the value our family places on academics. Her efforts to get good grades are just one choice of many that will dramatically shape her character as she commits to an individual identity in the next few years.

The influential psychologist Erik Erikson distinguished adolescence as a time when social norms and peers create havoc and confusion in the quest for identity.[8] As my daughter's comment indicates, teens balance developing their own traits, while also looking to fit in. They explore critical questions: Do I care about school and grades? Will I experiment with drugs and alcohol? How will I make my mark on the world? Peer pressure exerts its influence on the pursuit for personality and character, and, all too often during the teenage years, friends win out.

In the twenty-first century, typical identity exploration takes place online as well as in the real world. Children test the waters with social media; they post pictures and share aspects of their lives, waiting for a reaction from their peers. These reactions to their posts—which picture is liked, which gets more comments—will influence the next post. While the exploration is in the virtual world, the identity being shaped is all too real.

Desire for Popularity

Why do teenagers care so much about popularity? The constant drive to dominate the social order is portrayed in movie and television content such as *Mean Girls* and *Gossip Girl.* While everyone wants to be liked, the desire is on hyperdrive during this life stage.

Social scientists who study teens point to several reasons that underscore the intensity of this need. First, the peer group becomes a powerful force for social learning. Children begin to realize that their parents have a separate worldview that may not be relevant for a younger person.[9] Second, many children leave the comfort of their elementary school and enter into larger, less personal learning environments, and this transition can lead to a confused search for one's place.[10] In the chaotic and scary world of middle school, small groups feel safer, and being included in the groups with status becomes crucial.

Because kids don't have the life experience to understand that good grades can translate into future earnings, or that creative energy (e.g., theatre and band) might turn into artistic success, they find the most easily identifiable markers, and often least sophisticated, to chase popularity. Looks and money are tangible and simple to interpret; these symbols demonstrate status, both offline and on. Social networks allow adolescents to observe the behavior of their peers from a distance. They pay close to attention to followers and the number of likes on their friends' photos. These relatively straightforward signs point to popularity. Unfortunately, the superficial frequently wins out, just like it did when we were kids, but it's more noticeable and widespread online.

Peer Contagion

Peer contagion makes adolescents particularly susceptible to the problem behavior of their friends.[11] Adolescents in groups tend to influence one another as they engage in relationship behaviors to look for approval and companionship. Thanks to peer contagion, kids watch more confident peers and imitate their behavior, and soon the herd follows. Contagion is a useful metaphor for describing the influence of social networks on teen behavior. While poor decisions and destructive behavior are influential enough in the real world, online they are downright infectious.

These social factors during adolescence can impact health and development. During this critical time period, when children are particularly susceptible to peer influence, the digital environment could affect an insecure child's self-esteem and well-being.

Likes, Comments, and Views = Extrinsic Rewards

Psychologists delineate two kinds of rewards that encourage people. The first, popularized by Daniel Pink's best-selling novel *Drive*, is an intrinsic reward, which is intangible and internal. To understand this concept, consider what excites you, something you enjoy doing without a goal of money, a trophy, or accolades from your community. You do these activities because you are intrinsically motivated. By contrast, extrinsic rewards are a visible recognition of your work, such as grades, salaries, awards, and so forth. These kinds of rewards are embedded in schools, businesses, and workplaces.

The creators of social networks are clued into this basic human motivator. These media use extrinsic rewards; likes, comments, and views are subtle cues that offer incentives to continue your online activity. Recognition in the online world feels good. As you post pictures or status updates online, you receive encouraging affirmation from others. The carrots entice and keep us returning for more rewards.

A fascinating fMRI study conducted in Germany found concrete proof, on the neural level, that the design features of social media act as an extrinsic motivator.[12] The scientists' hypothesis was that Facebook use would be related to receiving positive feedback on postings. The researchers examined the college-age participants' brains and measured the activity in their reward circuitry, the area of the brain that responds to tangible compensation such as receiving money. When the subjects received likes or comments on a post with their photo, this area lit up.

The researchers also found that the neural activity in the reward area was stronger for those people who used social media more frequently. The implication is that, as you post pictures of yourself and receive positive feedback, you will want to use social media more. As the PBS *Frontline* documentary entitled "Generation Like" posits, "liking" may indeed be this generation's defining attribute. With the instant and public delivery of online reinforcement, we just might be encouraging a generation of young minds to crave the "like."

Capitalism at Work: Social Media = Big Business

I recently shopped online for a pair of tennis shoes for my daughter. Later, as I looked at various newspaper services while doing research for this book, ads for the shoes popped up. I was somewhat horrified; this kind of personalized ad feels intrusive and Big Brotherish. However, it's also a good reminder that nothing is truly free; the Internet must be paid for, and the ones paying for it are brands and businesses.

Marketers spend considerable energy studying what will appeal to preteens and teenagers in both the real and virtual world. By early adolescence, when materials goods become aligned with social status, children express preferences for brands and different shopping experiences. Research also finds that consumerism is higher in children who communicate with peers more frequently.[13]

It's no coincidence that the elements of social networking sites map onto typical teen desires. Our kids grow up immersed in an environment where their friends are available to them with the click of a button. Through social media, brands interact directly with teenagers and their friends, outside the purview of adults. Retailers that target teens use impression management to influence perceptions and invite social comparison by placing online or mobile ads that feature attractive actors using their merchandise. These ads, which constantly show up in feeds, court likes with giveaways and other features. If the brand is accepted, peer contagion gives it a further boost.

As adults, we need to remember that the revenue growth of online social media companies is spurred by aggregating data and audience in order to sell product. Online communities, where children practice social learning and develop youth identity, are owned and operated by major corporations that push image and status conferred by audience size and likes as a means of selling their product. In this kind of community, a superficial image often becomes one's defining feature, and when you are in the throes of building identity, the marketplace, through satisfying developmental needs for popularity and belongingness, may be shaping that identity and influencing developing value systems.[14]

Fifteen Minutes in the Digital Age

As Andy Warhol declared in the 1960s, everyone wants his fifteen minutes of fame. In 2014, those fifteen minutes became six seconds, the length of a Vine video. The quest for renown is natural, but for most of our history, fame was associated with accomplishment in a particular arena—art, politics, music, science, etc. Since the advent of social media and reality television, fame has been linked with typical human behavior, and all too often, the worse the behavior, the more attention the person receives. The *Real Housewives* series, *Keeping Up with the Kardashians*, and *16 and Pregnant* have all made celebrities of their stars, who are rewarded with numerous magazine covers and social media followers. Fame seems attainable to the ordinary person; you may not need a special talent. Accordingly, hundreds of thousands of young people hope for its rewards.

Television—A Reflection of Culture

I noticed a change in the television landscape when I watched the hit series *Hannah Montana* on Disney with my then nine-year-old daughter. As I started graduate school, I decided to test whether my hypothesis—that TV shows for children portrayed fame as achievable for kids—was based on a bona fide trend or on a yearning for the programming of my youth.

I conducted my study with my advisor at the Children's Digital Media Center@LA (CDMC@LA) at UCLA; we compared the top two shows for tweens in one year of every decade starting in 1967.[15] I suspected that fame would be an important feature in the two top shows of 2007—*American Idol* and *Hannah Montana*—but was surprised to find that fame was at the bottom of the list in every other decade. Just ten years earlier, fame was not an important aspiration. What could have changed so drastically in such a short span of time?

Top Two Shows for Tweens in CDMC@LA study

	1967	1977	1987	1997	2007
Survey 1	Andy Griffith	Laverne and Shirley	Growing Pains	Sabrina the Teenage Witch	American Idol
Survey 2	The Lucy Show	Happy Days	Alf	Boy Meets World	Hannah Montana

Note: Source of Nielsen ratings: 1967 and 1977: wikipedia.com and fiftiesweb.com; 1987 and 1997: CBS records; 2007: usatoday.com and cable360.net.

As my advisor and I explored the reasons for our findings, we looked to notable changes in the environment. Internet use rocketed from 70 million worldwide users in 1997 to 1.3 billion in 2007. More significantly, Facebook began in 2004 and YouTube followed in 2005. Could the values portrayed on television be reflecting these changes? As I continued to investigate the media landscape, I remembered the highly rated Nickelodeon series *iCarly,* about two high school girls who created a popular online program and in the process became famous. Their fame translated to popularity at their school, with kids, and even adults such as the principal, begging to be on the program. Here's what Dan Schneider, the creator of this show and many other popular Nickelodeon series, said in an article in the *Los Angeles Times*: "If there is anything I've learned about kids today—and I'm not saying this is good or bad—it's that they all want to be stars."[16]

As we explored our findings further in focus group studies with fourth and sixth graders, we discovered that children did indeed connect these messages to the TV programming they loved.[17] Moreover, they knew that teen celebrities such as Justin Bieber and Rebecca Black used YouTube to launch their careers. I came to believe that these television programs, in the business of getting eyeballs on screens, merely captured what was in the zeitgeist—more kids becoming famous at younger ages using the tools of the Internet. As a result, art was imitating life, not the other way around.

Hollywood has always glamorized being rich and famous, yet we do seem to be living in a unique epoch. The Brat Pack ruled Hollywood in the 1980s, but those celebrities were just a handful of kids. Today, teen idols are inescapable, and because the media love youth, we see them everywhere, on television, in movies, and online. And kids notice and idealize these role models.

The Path to Online Fame

#AlexfromTarget began the path to fame when a British girl posted a photo on Tumblr of Alex bagging groceries during his day job. As it goes, the photo went viral. The sixteen-year-old boy from Texas went on to be featured on ABC TV and *Ellen;* he currently boasts 740,000 followers on Twitter and 2.2 million on Instagram. My daughter and her friends, far from Texas, know everything about him and think he is hot (their words, not mine). He is still working at Target.

So far it seems that Alex is not using his fame to build a career in the limelight. However, media stories like his inspire many other teens and young adults to slog away trying to turn themselves into a brand. And why not? Clicks, likes, and followers can turn into money.

In 2015, the gatekeepers are no longer in sole power: anyone can post a video or write an article and reach an audience. While the Hollywood studios I used to work for scramble to redefine their business models, millennials like Mark Zuckerberg and Evan Spiegel rapidly invent platforms that take away the studios' power.

Noting the decline of traditional media, the trendspotter Ypulse declared that YouTube is the New Hollywood. Even the passe trade magazine *Daily Variety* wrote that the five most popular celebrities for kids are YouTube stars. The more YouTube videos people watch, the more money the company makes. Click a button, and Google will place ads on your channel—and in the process collect 45 percent of the proceeds.[18]

Yet, to reach true celebrity status you must be persistent and work tirelessly, and success is far from guaranteed. Only a few of YouTube's "celebrities" earn a good living. The advertising dollars are spread among so many people posting video content that most make nothing.

Moreover, banking on a future based on viral content is stressful and comes with pressure and scrutiny that many are unprepared to handle. The creator of the video *Kony 2012*, which was watched by more than seventy million people in less than a week, notably went temporarily insane. If an adult succumbs to this kind of pressure, a teen with a fragile developing identity, would surely be affected.

Extreme Cases

Children who pursue attention and an audience often don't have the maturity to understand the costs. At the extreme end of the spectrum, mentally unstable people could use violent methods to achieve fame. While many other factors are certainly in play when those types of devastating events occur, even a dumb prank can turn ugly. For example, I was asked to comment on MSNBC on the actions of a young girl who sent this tweet: "@AmericanAir hello my name's Ibrahim and I'm from Afghanistan. I'm part of Al Qaida and on June 1st I'm gonna do something really big bye."

American Airlines took her threat seriously and reported it to the FBI, and she was arrested. But her initial reaction to the attention she received was, "My terrorist tweet is in my bio lol" and "Omg I got over 10K rts for that tweet omg" (rt = retweets) and "over 20K followers yay." Unbelievably, this foolish young woman was more focused on her instant fame than on the consequences of her actions.

FOMO (Fear of Missing Out)

You are missing out if you haven't heard about FOMO, an affliction made for the digital age. FOMO is not new; the anxiety one feels over the comparison of one's own social life to another's is the curse and luxury of a modern lifestyle.

When I was a teen, if I suffered the indignity of being at home with my family on a Saturday night, I definitely worried about missing out on all the fun. On Monday morning at school, I heard about the party that I imagined that everyone else except me attended. Those experiences were pretty depressing, but my children have it worse. During this life stage, when social inclusion and exclusion are of paramount concern, the tools of social media can be devastating to some children, giving them little escape from the anxiety of "missing out."[19]

Unfortunately, for kids today the angst of missing out is interminable. On social media, excluded children witness friends living glamorous lives in exotic locales in real time, which allows FOMO to fester. Girls, in particular, are subject to these social pressures; a survey of thirteen- to eighteen-year-old children, primarily girls, found that they worry more about FOMO than about fitting in.[20]

The public nature of today's social media promotes social comparison, and it is all too easy to feel inadequate. Feelings of FOMO can lead to obsessive anxiety, and for some children, these feelings are overwhelming.

Selfies

In 2009 we shared 50 million photos daily; in 2014, that number was 1.8 billion. What could have changed in just five years? There's no doubt that the rise of the selfie, which the *Oxford Dictionary* declared the word of the year in 2013 after its usage spiked 17,000 percent, contributed to the photography boom. If you are living under a rock, here is that dictionary's definition of a selfie: "A photograph that one has taken of oneself, typically one taken with a smartphone or webcam and shared via social media."

According to a March 2014 Pew Research Center poll, more than half of all millennials took a selfie and shared it online. This generation's obsession with its own image seems excessive, but parents contribute to the culture by sharing online photos and videos of kids from birth. Moreover, many of the toys we give young children have cameras that teach them to take their own pictures. For example, handheld portable gaming devices come with cameras that feature a simple button that lets the user take his own picture. One mobile that hangs above a baby's crib will take a picture when he kicks it and then post it automatically on a website.

When I was a high school student, I took my first photography class. My teacher taught me to point my Nikon camera at subjects in my environment and to frame those photos for maximum impact. I was assigned a self-portrait, of course, but it was not easy to take this kind of photo. I had to find a tripod and turn the camera to face me, using the timer to snap the picture.

Most of the time, however, I used the camera to explore other people's perspectives. I was particularly proud of the photo I took of an angry man selling balloons in front of Filene's Basement in Boston. By spending my creative energy reflecting on others rather than myself, I learned to put myself in another's shoes and to imagine that person's perspective.

In the last few years, the meaning of photography has fundamentally changed; instead of taking pictures of other people and landscapes, we focus more on our own reflection and experience. It's a stark contrast to our recent past, when photography reflected the world beyond us. This transformation could challenge a developing identity.

Once children can share their self-photos online, they post them incessantly, hoping for an immediate reaction. As a teen receives more comments and likes on a particularly attractive photo, others in their social circle notice, and their status increases. "So pretty," one writes; soon after, another comments, "You look so pretty"; and then the comments come rolling in, one after another: "so freakin cute," "ah, u look so pretty," and so on. Who wouldn't lust after these kinds of accolades?

The actor James Franco, who has been criticized for posting too many selfies, wrote an articulate piece for the *New York Times* on the allure of these photos:

> But a well-stocked collection of selfies seems to get attention. And attention seems to be the name of the game when it comes to social networking. In this age of too much information at a click of a button, the power to attract viewers amid the sea of things to read and watch is power indeed. It's what the movie studios want for their products, it's what professional writers want for their work, it's what newspapers want—hell, it's what everyone wants: attention. Attention is power.[21]

Think of the myth of Narcissus, who became obsessed with his own reflection, and the implication is clear. Some speculate that selfies could drive a demand for plastic surgery. Indeed, in 2013, 33 percent of surgeons reported that more of their patients were more aware of their looks due to social media.[22]

The selfie is normalized in our culture today. Unfortunately, children have no societal norms to stop them from hyperkinetically posting as they seek validation from their friends in the online world.

Wrap-Up and Takeaways

Wrap-Up of the Research

1. Basic psychological mechanisms are at play when we use social media.
2. Impression management, whereby we manage the way others see us, is in high gear when we are on social media. Social comparison to others is also ever present.

3. Adolescents are particularly sensitive to these mechanisms as they develop identity, seek popularity, and look to their peers. An immature sense of self puts one at risk for believing that everyone else's online and carefully managed image is accurate.
4. The stimulus of social media—likes, comments, and views—act as extrinsic rewards and motivate people in the same way.
5. Our culture, facilitated by these media, may be changing to be more self-focused. Fame, FOMO, and selfies are certainly challenging issues for some people, and they are exacerbated by the affordances of media.

Takeaways for Parents

1. Know your child. For the majority of children, the benefits of social media—fitting in, social learning, self-esteem—outweigh the costs.
2. If you suspect your child is having issues with social exclusion or has an unrealistic perception of her peers' lives, however, take extra care with her online activity. Monitor carefully.
3. Talk to your child about FOMO and the downside and difficulties of an online path to fame.
4. When you first give your child a camera and the means to post photos online, consider banning selfies. Ask him to only post photos of other people or his environment. Try it for a short time period.
5. Help your child notice posting behavior of his peers. For example, does someone dress a certain way, or only post selfies? Try to connect the dots as to what an online post may mean about offline personality and value systems.
6. Teach your children about the consumerism inherent in social media. Show them the link between what they post and the advertisements that pop up. Remind them that brands, such

as those in the ever-present beauty industry, can sometimes make us feel "less than" so we will buy their product.

7. If you want to help your child, and yourself, reflect on your online behavior, you could consider something like Think Up, an online subscription service that analyzes how you act on social media (it only looks at Twitter and Facebook). You can get a free fourteen-day trial.

PART THREE

Learning

CHAPTER 7

Learning in the Digital Age

[F]or this discovery of yours [writing] will create forgetfulness in the learners' souls, because they will not use their memories; they will trust to the external written characters and not remember of themselves.

—*Phaedrus*, fourth century BC

When the alphabet was invented several millennia ago, philosophers speculated that this new way of communicating would negatively affect memory. Humans were transitioning from an oral to a print culture, and the effects were unknown and worrisome. Without the need to remember, would memory be eroded? Plato wrote of these concerns in the play *Phaedrus*, yet he himself was a writer who benefited from the ability to set down his thoughts. I doubt many people today would argue that writing and reading were the downfall of civilization. Quite the contrary: without the written word, would we have advanced so far?

Similarly, in the third millennium, many people wonder how digital media and the Internet will affect our minds and learning. Some say that we are constantly distracted by the never-ending flow of information, while others claim that the ability to access any knowledge we need at any time, from around the globe, allows greater efficiency. While researchers explore the incremental changes in our cognition, parents continue to worry about the long-term effects. Social scientists are testing many hypotheses on multitasking, reading, memory, and more. The research moves slower than the technology but we are making progress.

Distraction: A By-Product of the Digital Age?

An extreme mobility of the attention...makes the child seem to belong less to himself than to every object that grabs his attention.

—William James, psychologist and philosopher, 1890

In the digital age, information is plentiful. The Global Information Industry Center at the University of California, San Diego, reports that the hours of information that Americans consume outside of work each day, grew from 7.4 hours per person in 1980 to 11.8 in 2008.[1] During the latter year, adults in the United States consumed information—from books, newspapers, video, and computers—a staggering 1.3 trillion hours in total; this corresponds to nearly twelve hours or 100,500 words per day, per person.

Yikes.

Every minute we are on the Internet, information is hurled at us. Business models are built around catching the consumer's attention, and distraction is built into most products. For instance, just this morning as I answered a private message in LinkedIn, a sidebar popped up, noting the new job of a former colleague. Of course I was curious and clicked on the link, and guess what? I immediately forgot to finish my correspondence.

It's no wonder we all feel overwhelmed, but is this is a new experience, caused by the digital age? And are our children, who know nothing but a world of instant gratification and endless distractions that are available by a click or tap, doomed to a life of divided focus? Alternatively, perhaps as the William James quote at the top of this chapter suggests, mobility of attention is simply part of childhood. Current and past social science research should help us determine what is new and what might simply be business as usual.

Too Many Screens, Too Hard to Focus?

A fascinating 2011 study filmed participants at a university as they simultaneously worked on a computer and watched television. The researchers found that people switched their focus between the two media four times per minute.[2] Could the distraction of multiple screens be responsible for the short attention spans?

A study from 1997 indicates otherwise. The researchers examined gaze duration while participants watched TV. They found that the average time their subjects focused on the television monitor was less than three seconds. No other diversion was in the vicinity of the television, yet participants only gave the program three seconds before they glanced away. Interestingly enough, in both studies, people were unable to sustain focus on the television for very long.

Check out the Google graph below, which shows how often the word "distraction" appeared in books over the last two hundred years. In 1800 the word showed up at the same percentage rate as it did in 2000. These examples seem to indicate that long before the Internet made information available 24–7, our minds would naturally wander.

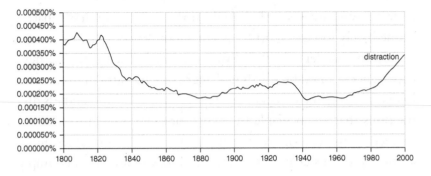

Source: Google Books Ngram Viewer[3]

Are Kids Becoming Distracted Learners?

Hundreds or thousands of variables affect attention. How would you know that the reason you can't focus or think deeply is because of Internet use? Factors that affect focus include temperament, age, hormones, or just a bad day. Every individual has different levels of focus and distractibility, and each is likely to be affected in varying manners. Without a rigorous experiment to measure how the Internet affects attention, one cannot conclude that the Internet *causes* distraction.

The reality is that we have little hard proof that this generation is any more distracted than we were. Instead of worrying about the effects of the mountains of digital information streams, teach your children to be aware of the manufactured online distractions. Consider the words of this teenage boy who wrote a popular article that detailed why he likes Instagram: "There are no links on Instagram, meaning I'm not being constantly spammed by the same advertisement, horrible gossip news article, or Buzzfeed listing about the "28 Ingenious Things For Your Dog You Had No Idea You Needed."[4] Remarkably, on his own, this nineteen-year-old found a way to avoid the diversions of marketers and sensationalists.

In practice, some kids are able to focus better than others; a kid who has difficulty focusing offline will be the one most challenged by the Internet's affordances. If your child cannot finish his homework and get the grades you expect, restrict his distractions.

> **Bottom Line:** Our attention spans were always limited, but the bombardment of information in the digital world provides many diversions. Teach your child to become aware of the many means by which their attention is distracted while they are online (e.g., incoming text sound, pop-up ads, etc.).

Multitasking

It was my daughter's fifteenth birthday, and I attempted five different conversations at once. How was this even humanly possible? Let me explain. Here is a list of each exchange:

1. Live chatting with the Comcast agent
2. Texting with my daughter's friend, who was planning a birthday event
3. Texting with my mother, who wrote to tell me she loved the birthday photo I sent
4. Holding on the phone to schedule a doctor's appointment
5. Yelling back and forth with my husband, who was in another room

To top it all off, I was baking a cake.

Due to the asynchronous nature of mediated communication, I could use every single pause in the back-and-forth moments of "conversation" to accomplish another task. The virtual world allowed me to be superhuman: two conversations were on my mobile phone; one was on the computer; another took place on a landline; and only one was with a live human being. The extreme

balancing act made me feel very virtuous. My multitasking capabilities were in high gear. I was a modern woman, having it all.

Multitasking used to mean productivity and accomplishment.
But these days, it has a negative connotation as we watch our
teens toggle back and forth through multiple screens at once. I
get anxious when my daughter sends a Snapchat with her smartphone while she "reads" on her iPad and watches a Netflix video
on her computer screen. Yet I wonder if I am being hypocriti-
cal? When I use my own devices to accomplish several tasks at
once, I feel productive, but I judge her to be wasting her life away
looking at screens.

I am not alone in my judgment. Recent news headlines include:

"Don't Multitask: Your Brain Will Thank You"
                        —*Time* magazine, April 17, 2013

"You'll Never Learn! Students can't resist multitasking,
and it's impairing their memory."
                        —*Slate* magazine, May 3, 2013

When and how did a valued skill, something that mothers
do on a regular basis, turn into something negative? Media multitasking, distinct from traditional multitasking, is a relatively
new phenomenon. Survey research first uncovered the trend, and
children were early adopters.

The Emergence of the Media Multitasking Trend

I multitask every single minute I am online. At this very
moment I am watching TV, checking my e-mail every two
minutes, reading a newsgroup about who shot JFK, burning
some music to a CD, and writing this message.
                        —Kaiser study participant, 2006[5]

The Kaiser Family Foundation researchers who surveyed changes in the media habits of children over a period of ten years, from 1999 to 2009, were the first scientists to highlight the changing media habits of children. In 2005, they found that media multitasking—which they identified as using several screen-based media at the same time—was a new behavior for American children.[6] In the last year of the study, the research scientists estimated that children eight to eighteen years of age spent a mind-boggling eleven hours a day, seven days a week, using multiple media at once.[7]

Their findings led to enormous concern in the scientific community. In 2009, I attended a multidisciplinary gathering of experts at Stanford; the goals of this meeting were to review and set a research agenda for the impact of media multitasking on children's learning and development. Concerns included distraction, lack of focus, disappearance of downtime, and more.[8] Since that conference, multitasking has become more frequent, and while adults still worry, this pattern is more normalized in our culture.

For example, less than ten years ago, only 17 percent of youth reported that they media multitasked with television;[9] today, it's rare *not* to do so. In fact, marketers take advantage of the "second screen" and encourage people to tweet from phones and tablets while they watch event programming on television.

Meanwhile, multiple devices proliferate in our homes. Another significant question is whether we will we become more efficient at processing all the streams of information? Can humans really do two things just as effectively at the same time? Research on multitasking suggests we cannot.

Tap Your Head and Rub Your Belly

Attention is limited, and when we divide our attention between two activities, we automatically perform worse on one. The brain can only focus on one thing at a time, so we alternate between tasks.[10] When we multitask, we are in fact rapidly switching from one undertaking to the other. This takes a toll, because switching costs time. Our brain becomes bottlenecked as it figures out which activity to perform.[11] Thus, while you may believe you conduct several actions simultaneously, as I did on my daughter's birthday, in all reality, your attention is not equally divided. The time spent switching is often negligible, however, and sometimes, our full focus is not necessary to complete a chore.

> **Bottom Line:** You cannot do two things at the same time with identical attention. Some tasks don't require our undivided focus; in many cases, it is possible to *adequately* multitask.

The Myth of the Expert Media Multitasker

Several experts theorized that as young people spent more time balancing multiple media at once, they would become superhuman task switchers. However, a well-publicized study out of Stanford, still quoted in nearly every press article about multitasking, refuted this hypothesis.[12] The researchers asked 262 college students about their multitasking habits, and found that those who reported the *most* media multitasking performed the *worst* on a series of complicated assessments.

The scientists tested two groups of students: those who multitasked the most, a group of fifteen (designated "Heavy Multitaskers" [HMM]), and those who multitasked the least, another group of fifteen (LMM). Everyone else was recused from the experiment. Researchers next measured each group's ability to switch between two mentally challenging tasks.

To their surprise, the HMMs performed much worse than the LMMs. The lesser performance of the HMM group, students who were hyper accustomed to the concurrent use of multiple screens, was completely unexpected. After all, shouldn't practice make perfect?

A closer look at the study suggests a cautious interpretation of the results.[13] The tested groups were at extreme ends of the multitasking spectrum. Only 6 percent of the students were labeled HMM and another 6 percent were LMM. That leaves out 88 percent of the sample. In all likelihood the HMM students had other attention issues (e.g., ADHD prevalence rates are estimated at 9.5 percent in the United States and may have been a factor). The researchers themselves theorized that these kids, who believed they were quite capable of using multiple media at once, were instead easily distracted by irrelevant information in their surroundings. Despite the clever design of this study, more research is needed using a larger, more representative sample.[14]

> **Bottom Line:** It does not appear that kids who have more experience with media multitasking are better at it than those who do it less. However, more research is needed.

Does Schoolwork Suffer?

Most parents' chief concern with their child's media multitasking is how it affects her schoolwork. At the Children's Digital Media Center@LA (CDMC@LA) we tested the effects of multitasking on reading comprehension and memorization (described fully on page 138).[15] College students read several passages; one group had their phones, and another did not. We found that the students with phones scored at similar levels on the comprehension and memory tests as those with no distractions. However, it did take them longer to read the short essays.

Another study out of Connecticut State tested whether receiving instant messages while reading would affect a student's understanding. The findings of that study were similar to ours. It took more time for students to complete the reading, but their comprehension was not diminished. In both cases, the students absorbed what they needed to in order to make sense of the passage. The results suggest that if constrained time is not a factor, multitasking in itself should not affect reading performance.

What about a task that requires greater concentration? In another study completed for the CDMC@LA, also described in more detail below, we tested whether critical thinking would be affected by multitasking.[16] Students read several articles and wrote a one-page paper; one group had access to the Internet and the other did not. Students in the Internet group scored 63 percent; the non-multitasking group scored ten points higher, at 73 percent. Thus, for a more complicated task, such as one that requires critical thinking, multitasking is not ideal.

> **Bottom Line:** If time is not an issue, then some multitasking while completing reading assignments should not affect basic comprehension. For more challenging homework that requires deeper focus and conceptual understanding, multitasking should be discouraged.

Reading in the Digital Age

When I was in graduate school I read a shocking article by Marc Prensky called "Why YouTube Matters." Prensky is the provocateur who popularized the terms digital immigrant and native, and his premises are frequently thought provoking. He proclaimed that YouTube was the new text.[17] His prediction was that online video would transform education, and in the process eradicate reading for the masses.

Scary stuff to a parent who loves reading!

Prensky's argument had some merit. Reading, after all, became popularized only several hundred years ago; this represents a tiny fraction of human existence. He posited that the human brain evolved to process information visually, and since online video can be easily transmitted, we would return to evolutionary processes—learning through seeing. He further suggested that, since most people are visual learners, in the future text-based learning, the foundation of our educational system, will not be the norm.

Reading is indeed difficult for many people; in the U.S., most high school students can read books only at the fifth-grade level, and thirty-two million adults are illiterate. The well-known intellectual Howard Gardner theorized in his book *Multiple Intelligences* that each person is intelligent in different ways. If linguistic intelligence is only one of seven avenues through which we learn, then perhaps reading is not the only way to teach?

On the flip side, reading is one of the few media that allows perspective taking, a critical part of empathy. When we read a novel, we gain insight into a character's innermost thoughts. In audiovisual media such as fictional TV or movies, the storytelling mechanism is generally not expository; characters show, rather than tell, why they acted as they did. Similarly, on social media, we present ourselves in the best light, which means we may not be honest about what we feel. A recent study found a decline in empathy among young adults. If people are reading less in the digital age, could a relationship exist between the two?

Marc Prensky wrote the aforementioned essay in 2009, and in the ensuing years digital literacy became a heralded concept. Does it come at the expense of print literacy? Is reading indeed becoming a dinosaur habit? So far, the data indicates otherwise.

Did Video Kill the Reading Star?

In sharp contrast to Prensky's article and the provocative headlines, people read *more* than they used to. In 1949, Gallup polls
reported that 21 percent of American adults read books; in 2005
that number had more than doubled, to 47 percent![18] Interestingly, the people who read books the most are usually the ones
who love other media as well; 33 percent of people who do not
attend movies read books, but nearly double this amount, 62 percent, report doing both. It seems that people who love media and
storytelling enjoy it in multiple formats; watching videos and
reading books can go hand in hand.

What about children? While anecdotal evidence abounds that the
younger generation never reads, in 2014 the Pew Research Internet
Project surveyed Americans sixteen and over and found that teenagers actually read *more* than adults.[19] Eight-eight percent of the youth
reported that they had read a book in the last year, while only 79
percent of adults over thirty could say the same. It should be noted,
however, that these percentages include reading for work and school.

By contrast, the 2010 Kaiser survey of eight- to eighteen-year-
olds found that total time spent with print media decreased from
forty-three minutes a day to thirty-eight between 1999 and 2009.[20]
If one unpacks the study's findings, several factors undermine the
downfall-of-reading narrative. Time spent reading books, a subset of the total, rose from twenty-one to twenty-five minutes a
day. Magazine and newspaper reading drove the decrease, dropping from twenty-two minutes a day to twelve. And therein lies
an issue. When we measure reading on paper, statistics reflect a
decline, but when we factor in online reading, a different story
emerges. In fact, the same Kaiser report found that the kids who
read online magazines and newspapers spent twenty-one minutes
a day doing so. And recall the study from the Global Information
Industry Center at UC San Diego, which measured the number

of words we read per day: that study found a tripling in the number of words we read between 1980 and 2008. The reason? Text, rather than video, is still the preferred way to receive information on the Internet. Finally, studies report that, as with movies and reading, adults who use the Internet more also read more.

> **Bottom Line:** We read more than ever before. Thank you, Internet.

Early Language Learning

Reading on the Internet may in fact motivate preschoolers to learn language and vocabulary. An Australian study followed a group of young kids born in 1999 (beginning when they were four years old and ending when they were nine) and another cohort born in 2003 (ages zero to five).[21] The researchers measured how much the children read books, watched television, and used a computer. For the younger group, access to the Internet correlated with better verbal abilities. For the older kids, computers were also associated with a better mastery of vocabulary. However, the researchers cautioned that when children are under four, factors other than media use (and in particular television content, which they found did not influence vocabulary) are more influential on reading. Parental education and parents' participation in their child's media use were stronger considerations.

Paper Versus Screen

As more and more people begin to read on screens, for school and for pleasure, are we sacrificing anything beyond an emotional connection to paper?

Print Versus Screen

In the study our team at the CDMC@LA published, entitled "Learning from Paper, Learning from Screens: Impacts of Screen Reading and Multitasking Conditions on Reading and Writing Among College Students," the vast majority of the participants reported that they preferred studying on paper.[22] In the study, we explored whether reading on paper versus a screen would affect how much students understand and remember what they read. We also wondered if reading on either medium would make a difference in critical thinking, an important twenty-first-century skill. Would we find a screen or paper advantage?

In one of our studies, conducted at California State University, Los Angeles, students read two short passages, one easy and one hard, on a laptop, a tablet, or paper. Surprisingly, no matter how they read, on paper or on screen, students performed similarly on tests of comprehension and memory of the excerpts.

In a second experiment, run on the UCLA campus, the participants were asked to create an evidence-based opinion report, something they did for school on a regular basis. In two groups, participants read seven articles on either paper or a computer screen, with contrasting information on the topic of ADHD. After reading the seven articles, each participant prepared a one-page paper (using Microsoft Word on the computer) synthesizing and articulating his opinion on the best course of action. In the analysis phase of the research, an assistant and I "graded" the papers. We were "blind" to condition; neither of us knew in which format the students had read the article. Whether they read the articles on screens or paper, their grades did not significantly differ.

> Bottom line: Many outcomes such as memory, comprehension, and even critical thinking are the same whether you read on paper or screen.

Reading to Your Child—Print Book or E-Book?

When my children were young I had one way to read to them, from an old-fashioned print book. Today, parents can read to their kids using a variety of platforms, and many take advantage of the options. For instance, in a Common Sense Media survey, the percentage of parents who reported reading to children on mobile devices grew from just 4 percent in 2011 to 30 percent in 2013.[23]

The bells and whistles on interactive storybooks are alluring, but research finds that these features may distract from reading comprehension. In a study published in 2013, 165 parents, paired with a child aged three or five, read either from a Fisher-Price Power Touch Electronic Console (EC) system or a printed book.[24] They found that when reading to their children on the EC, parents used fewer techniques that encourage story comprehension and reading skill. In a follow-up study, the researchers found that three-year-olds who read from a traditional book remembered more about the content and sequence of events than those kids who read from an EC book.

> **Bottom Line:** Go old-school when reading books to young children.

Writing Longhand Versus Typing

What about penmanship? Do we really need it?

Many parents lament that we are losing our handwriting skills, and wonder whether this harms the academic learning of the next generation. Scientists from the University of Pennsylvania and UCLA decided to test whether taking notes on computer was less effective than taking them by hand.[25] When you take notes by hand, because it is impossible to get every word down, you must sometimes paraphrase, which means you have to spend time processing the content of what you are writing. Two processes occur— you encode the information in your brain and store it on the paper.

By contrast, when you type during a lecture, you tend to transcribe the words efficiently (storage), but don't always process the information (encoding). This type of note taking strives for verbatim transcription.

The researchers asked college students to watch TED Talks and take notes on either their laptops or paper. When quizzed after the class on the basic facts of the video, both groups performed equally well, but when asked a more sophisticated question that measured conceptual understanding, those who used handwriting trumped those who'd taken notes on the computer.

In another experiment, more closely reflecting real life, scientists gave students a week to study their notes before taking a test. Astoundingly, even though the students who'd typed their notes had more information to draw from, the students who'd used handwriting performed better on *both* the factual and the conceptual test. In a world where critical thinking is more important than recall and fact memorizing, conceptual understanding of materials is the gold standard of learning.

Ultimately, the authors believe that the students who used computers suffered because they did not take the time to process the content of the TED Talk. Perhaps if they were able to slow down, listen, and paraphrase as they typed, the differences between laptop and longhand would disappear. For those people like myself with handwriting that is nearly indecipherable, that is a relief.

Bottom Line: If your child takes notes in class on a computer, encourage him to summarize the lecture rather than type it exactly.

Does Texting Hurt Writing Skills?

Mobile technology fundamentally changed the way people communicate. Growing up, our dominant modes of communication with friends were letters, phone, and face-to-face interaction. Kids now send and receive about thirty texts a day every single day of the week.[26] Even with the rise of photo-driven apps like Snapchat and Instagram, texting is still one of the most prevalent way that teenagers use media to communicate.

Teens type acronyms into their phones as though they are bilingual. BRB (Be Right Back). CU (See You). MOS (Mom over Shoulder). The symbols they use seem like a secret language to parents. Except the second language is spoken through only one medium—mobile phones—and primarily with one cohort—peers.

Most parents do not believe that texting is writing; it's too informal, and grammar is clearly not a priority. Some teachers, however, love and appreciate that children write in this format, as they believe it inspires creativity and self-expression. Research can help us untangle the effects of texting—does it help develop writing skills or not?

A comprehensive report out of the United Kingdom, published in 2009, explored the texting habits of British preteens.[27] The researchers spent many years examining the relationship between the frequency of texting, written language, and verbal and nonverbal reasoning skills. At first glance, their results suggested that texting hurt writing; children who sent more texts performed worse on the verbal and nonverbal reasoning test. However, as they continued to conduct more research, they expanded their definitions and looked at the myriad ways that kids text as well as at other writing outcomes. After many additional years of in-depth analysis, they concluded that knowledge and use of "textisms" contributed to improved reading scores and other literacy skills. In other words, texting helped kids in their ability to read and write, not the reverse.

Bottom Line: Texting will not hurt writing proficiency, and, in fact, may encourage literacy and creative writing.

Is the Internet Affecting Memory?

Plato theorized that memory would decline as we shifted from an oral to a print culture, and today adults fret about the impact of our newest technology on our remembrance of things past. Whenever possible, humans find shortcuts to protect our cognitive capabilities. If we don't need to memorize something because we know we can access the information somewhere else, we won't. It's adaptive and smart to do so because this strategy allows our brains to focus on solving other problems. By treating computers and other digital devices as extensions of memory, people may be protecting themselves from the costs of forgetting while taking advantage of the benefits. A remarkable paper published in 2011 in *Science* magazine disclosed that we do indeed outsource our memory to the search engine Google.[28]

This elegant study, entitled "Google Effects on Memory: Cognitive Consequences of Having Information at our Fingertips," asked whether access to information through computers affects a person's recall. The researchers asked their subjects to type trivia statements into a computer. Half the people believed that the computer would save the information, and the other half believed it would be erased. When the participants thought the information would be erased, they remembered it; when they thought it would be saved, they didn't. Makes sense, right? Why would you attempt to retain information that is easily retrievable whenever you need it?

In a follow-up test, the scientists found their participants remembered *where* they stored the information more easily than *what* the information was. In other words, they remembered the file where the content was located but not the specifics of the information in the file. Logical. As long as you know where to find your document, and you know it will always be there when you need it, why spend mental energy memorizing its contents? Computers have become like the trusty assistant, significant other, or friend who remembers people's names for you. Come to think of it, can they invent an app for that?

Wrap-Up and Takeaways

Wrap-Up of the Research

1. Attention is limited, and when we divide our attention between two activities, we automatically perform worse on one.
2. For most tasks, the costs of multitasking will be time. If time constraints are not present, multitasking is not always deleterious, and basic comprehension and memorization for reading should not be compromised.
3. More challenging undertakings that require conceptual understanding will most likely be affected by the inherent distraction of paying attention to several things at once.
4. In the digital age, we read more than ever before, and teens read more books than adults (perhaps because of school assignments).
5. Reading on the Internet improves language learning in young children.
6. It makes no difference in memory, comprehension, nor critical thinking whether you read materials on screen or paper.
7. Writing notes by hand versus typing them improves understanding of the subject matter.
8. Texting does not appear to harm writing skills. In fact, it may improve creative writing.
9. We memorize less when we know we can save the information on a computer. When we have the choice, we will better

remember where we saved the file we need than the content in the file. Memory itself does not appear to be declining; instead, we shift what we memorize to take advantage of the capabilities of computers.

Takeaways for Parents

1. Some media multitasking, even while doing homework, is fine.
2. If homework requires deeper thinking (e.g., writing an essay), children should be separated from their Internet-connected devices.
3. Computer activity positively impacts reading because a great deal of the content online involves words.
4. Your kids should be encouraged to write anywhere and anyhow; even texting can improve their skills. Try to engage them in thinking creatively as you communicate with them on mobile devices.
5. It is fine for an older child to read on tablets, computers, or paper. Individual preferences should guide the choice (e.g., my daughter will only read paper books, my son only reads on his Kindle).
6. When reading to children on an electronic device, make sure to engage with them as you would when reading a traditional book. For example, comment on the story and ask them to relate the story to their own lives. Don't let them get too distracted by the sounds and buttons.
7. Teach your child to be strategic and thoughtful about how she processes information. If she types her lecture notes, suggest that she paraphrase rather than take down the teacher's words verbatim.
8. Know your kid and his preferences. Unless his grades are suffering, trust in your child's ability to adapt to the digital age.

CHAPTER 8

Education in the Digital Age

I am committed to working with this amazing Board of Education for finding a way to place a tablet in the hands of every student and school staff member...in the next 15 months.
—Former LAUSD Supertintendant John Deasy, 2012[1]

The superintendent of the second-largest school district in the nation had a radical notion—give a tablet to every single student in the Los Angeles Unified School District (LAUSD). All told, more than 640,000 students, from kindergarten to twelfth grade, would receive a tablet. Dr. John Deasy's argument was one of civil rights: hand the students their own devices, and the digital divide would decrease. Instantly, every kid would have the opportunity for unlimited information and learning. He pointed to the many other school districts and private schools that had closed their computer labs and gone one to one (i.e., one laptop or tablet per child). The kids in Los Angeles deserved the same. Kids from disadvantaged backgrounds would finally have the tools required to succeed in the twenty-first century.

When the first group of teachers received their iPads, newspapers reported that these educators were ready to make use of this fantastic new tool in their classrooms. Soon after, a press conference was arranged at the Broadacres Avenue Elementary School in

Educational Terminology

Pedagogy: The method and practice of teaching.

One to one: Programs that provide each student with her own digital device, usually tablets or laptops, in order to integrate the use of technology into day-to-day classroom activities.

Blended learning: Programs that teach students partly at supervised school sessions and partly through online delivery, with some element of student control over time, place, path, and/or pace of learning.

Sage on the stage: Shorthand for a traditional teaching method that places the teacher front and center, as the expert. Most classrooms are set up to maximize this framework, with desks facing forward, oriented toward the teacher.

Personalized instruction/learning: The idea that students have different learning styles and competencies, and that individual learning needs should be made a priority. The term is often used to tout the advantages of online learning, whereby a student can move at his own pace, advancing more slowly or quickly than he would in a classroom setting.

STEM learning (science, technology, engineering, and math): Fields of study identified as important for the future workforce. Educators are encouraged to engage their students in these subject matters.

Twenty-first-century skills: The knowledge needed to succeed both in school and outside of school. These skills include critical thinking, communication, collaboration, and creativity.[2]

Carson, where photographers snapped photos of smiling children holding up their iPads, thrilled about future opportunities.

Within three days, district efforts were derailed, as kids, curious and technologically savvy, broke through the software filter meant to keep them "safe." The program came to a grinding halt, the press had a field day, and the administrators of the program scrambled to do damage control with the public. But it was too late; the project was doomed and never recovered.

Not only was the program stopped, the superintendent stepped down from his job. In a Shakespearean twist, the FBI seized all files related to the project, and reporters speculated that Apple and Pearson, the software provider for the tablets, had colluded with the district to secure the unprecedented multiyear contract, which brought millions of dollars into their companies.

I must admit that when I heard about Dr. Deasy's proposal, I was skeptical. I spoke to numerous heads of schools in Los Angeles, and we wondered why the superintendent felt such an urgent need to put a tablet into every child's hands, even kindergarten students who could barely read. As a mother, I worried that bringing more devices into my children's lives during their dedicated formal learning time would be distracting. However, I also admired Dr. Deasy's tenacity and his desire to help underprivileged children in the district to learn how to use technology to access knowledge and develop twenty-first-century skills. In the end, however, it is not surprising that the project collapsed; it was rushed, and schools, and more importantly teachers, were not adequately prepared.

Is Technology the Magic Bullet?

Along with the curriculum changes came a new technology—programmed instruction, audio-visual equipment, classroom television, computers—which freed schools from the idea that one teacher standing before a class of 30 children was the ideal form of instruction.

—*Time* magazine, 1965

In the past decade or so, reformers have pushed technology as a fresh and innovative way to motivate children to learn. Yet this vision is not really a twenty-first-century phenomenon; computers were placed in classrooms for many decades before the turn of the new millennium.[3] In fact, Apple started its highly successful educator's program in 1984, long before the exponential growth of the Internet and the advent of mobile devices.

Nevertheless, in 2015, most educators agree that our current pedagogical models must be adapted to prepare students to compete in the global marketplace. The United States is falling behind in the worldwide race for higher test scores. The Internet allows personalized learning, critical in overcrowded classrooms where teachers cannot tend to the needs of every student. Moreover, technological know-how is crucial for many future careers: *Forbes* magazine reports that software developers are in high demand,[4] and my friends who work at Google and Netflix tell me that qualified engineers are impossible to find.

Two behemoth companies, Apple and Google, lead the national conversation about the future of educational technology. Apple's education webpage features gorgeous and inspiring photos of students who utilize the power of technology to reach their full learning potential. Engage, inspire, create, learn. The promise is clear—these brand new, exciting tools will transform the classroom.

With the pressure to improve test scores and to better prepare kids for the future workplace, more schools and districts buy in to this vision. In 2013, Apple sold eight million iPads to educational facilities around the world. Schools and educators across the country proudly display their partnership with the corporation with banners touting they are "Apple Distinguished." With iPads and laptop carts, as well as a suite of products and services to support the devices, Apple's expertise cannot be denied.

Google is now a formidable challenger to Apple's dominance in this arena. Google Chromebooks, less expensive and more closely analogous to the kinds of computers used by the majority of the global workforce, seems poised to tip the applecart (pun intended). In 2014, Google sold one million of its Chromebooks to schools. Increasingly, educators become proficient on the platform Google for Education, which includes productivity tools, products, and training. Résumés of technology coordinators state that they are "Google certified," which means they know how to use Google's educational products. Google's advantage of cost savings, along with the fact that it is, well... Google... makes it a force to be reckoned with.

The investment in technology is enormous, and comes with real opportunity costs. As a case in point, one New York school district kept teacher salaries flat and cut repairs to schools, while increasing spending on technology.[5] The stakes are high: invest in these programs and sacrifices must be made.

No one doubts that learning to use technology is an important element of twenty-first-century skills. Those children who are digitally literate will have an upper hand in the workforce. Yet well-funded corporations driven by profit and market forces may not always have our kids' best interests at heart. Their shiny presentations leave frazzled administrators with more choices, and greater confusion, about how best to proceed.

In addition, many parents are unsure about the best path to technological modernization. When my children were in elementary school, our parent association held many tense meetings about the best technology plan for the school. The parents argued for months. The many valid and important questions included:

1. Our children already spend too much time outside of school with media; is it really necessary for them to do their homework and school reading on these devices?
2. If educators focus too much on technology in the classroom, what other skills will be shortchanged?
3. On the other hand, shouldn't children learn the basic skills for using technology productively and creatively, to help them be more effective in college and in the job market?

In order to begin to answer questions about what makes the most sense for your child's school, let's consider carefully the current models for computer use in schools, as well as any data pointing to their effectiveness, or lack thereof.

One-to-One Programs

LAUSD's superintendent was determined that every child in the district would have her own tablet. However, is it really necessary to give each enrolled child her own device beginning in kindergarten? Certainly, putting devices into a classroom setting seems more organic to practical academic instruction than segregating computers in one area of the school. Moreover, in the real world, we don't go to separate "computer labs" to do the parts of our job that require technology. However, most public schools are cash strapped; are one-to-one programs a good use of their budgets?

Some studies find benefits to these programs, but often the measures are limited to self-reports, with inherently subjective variables such as "student engagement." In addition, it takes time for a program's effects to emerge; in the first year, technological complications, such as adequate wireless bandwidth, must be resolved. More importantly, teachers need extensive training to get up to speed. In order to effectively examine this enormous investment, evidence from long-term one-to-one programs provides important information. The programs listed below, which were in place for more than ten years, suggest proceeding cautiously.

Maine Learning Technology Initiative

In the fall of 2002, the state of Maine began the Maine Learning Technology Initiative (MLTI), a program designed to put laptops into the hands of every middle school student in Maine. All seventh- and eighth-grade students and teachers in the state received an Apple MacBook, paid for with tax dollars.

MLTI was the brainchild of Angus King, who was governor of Maine at the time. The program was controversial and expensive. The governor was determined, however, and through his sheer will, funding was approved each year, even though the end result was uncertain. It was not until 2012 that a group of researchers from the Maine Education Policy Research Institute and the University of Southern Maine published a comprehensive assessment of the bold initiative.

The study, commissioned by the state legislature, reported a few positive results phrased as "significant impact on curriculum."[6] However, other news was not as favorable. Only a minority of the students reported that they used their computers more than four hours a week. The teachers tended to use the laptops to teach science, social studies, and English, but math teachers reported using them less frequently.

Significantly, the program did not affect students' test scores. Even after a decade of laptops in the hands of every child and teacher, in the 2013–2014 school year, Maine's state achievement indicators for math and English were nearly identical to the United States's average. Still, Angus King, now a U.S. senator, is proud of his achievement. However, by most accounts, MLTI is considered to be a costly program with unclear outcomes.

One Laptop per Child

The charming founder of the Massachusetts Institute of Technology (MIT) Media Lab, Nicholas Negroponte, had a vision. He wanted to provide laptops to children for use at home and school in some of the poorest countries in the world. The theory behind the program was that a laptop would transform the lives of these children and their families. Negroponte successfully sold his vision to funders, and in 2002, the One Laptop per Child (OLPC) program began. Below is the program's hopeful mission statement.

> To create educational opportunities for the world's poorest children by providing each child with a rugged, low-cost, low-power, connected laptop with content and software designed for collaborative, joyful, self-empowered learning. When children have access to this type of tool they get engaged in their own education. They learn, share, create, and collaborate. They become connected to each other, to the world and to a brighter future.[7]

Over ten years, more than two million laptops were distributed, and in 2012 the claims in the mission statement were tested. Research found that the donated laptops did not improve traditional academic learning such as math and language.[8] On the other hand, they did positively affect more general, though not specifically defined, "cognitive skills." Sadly, the program is now considered a failure.

Final Word on One to One

The stories above reflect a pattern that researchers who study digital technology in the classroom witness repeatedly: a high level of enthusiasm for the new technology, anecdotal stories about the transformational learning that will occur, an introduction along with many unanticipated challenges, and finally an investigation of the facts and effects.[9] Too often, the financial burden of the programs means drastic cutting in other arenas.

Convincing data does not back the claim that simply handing computers to kids will increase their engagement and achievement in academic subjects. The evidence is overwhelmingly clear that without adequate infrastructure and trained teachers, digital devices cannot meet their promise. As the report on the OLPC program concluded, "computers by themselves, at least as initially delivered by the program, do not increase achievement in curricular areas."

Other Forms of Technology Integration in the Classroom

While digital media should be part of modern pedagogy, other means of technology integration can be considered before a school commits to investing in a one-to-one program.

The Interactive Whiteboard

In the mid-nineteenth century, an educational technology was introduced to classrooms. Quickly adopted, it was widely praised. In fact, this technology is still in classrooms in the twenty-first century. What is this enduring tool? The chalkboard, of course.

An interactive whiteboard—perhaps the best-known brand is the SMART Board—is an electronic version of the chalkboard; these boards have large screens that are connected to a computer and a projector. Interactive whiteboards are cool; they have gigantic touchscreens, and even special pens. However, at five thousand dollars per unit, they are expensive, especially given that laptops and tablets can now easily project onto a screen.

As with other devices, teachers must be trained on how to

set up interactive whiteboards and use them productively in their lesson plans. However, for most educators, the interactive whiteboard is a more familiar tool than a tablet or computer. The chalkboard served students and teachers well for hundreds of years; the interactive whiteboard takes that technology into the digital age.

Blended Learning

Blended learning is an emerging pedagogy that combines both technology and old-school face-to-face instruction. In classrooms that support blended learning, students learn in both an online and a brick-and-mortar setting. This method allows for the efficiencies and personalization of online instruction while retaining the interaction and guidance of an in-person instructor. Different classroom models exist, but most rotate students through small group instruction and individual computer stations.

Hard data on blended learning academic outcomes for K–12 students is still scarce. However, a case study of the Blended Learning for Alliance School Transformation (BLAST), a group of middle and high schools in Los Angeles that serve an economically disadvantaged community (i.e., 96 percent participate in the free meal programs), shows promise. In 2010, these underserved schools determined that a blended learning pedagogy would benefit their students. The program expanded rapidly to cover three more high schools and five middle schools. In the classes, students learn through teacher-led small group instruction, individualized online lessons, and collaborative learning. Case studies of other charter school networks such as LA's KIPP: Empower Academy and New Orlean's FirstLine charter schools are also experimenting with this model with positive results and plans to expand to other schools within their networks. In the KIPP schools, for example, students significantly improved their reading scores, and while multiple factors contributed to this increase, their staff point to blended learning as an important pillar of their model for success.[10]

Maker Labs

The promise of maker labs, where people can use new technologies and equipment they may not otherwise have access to, is exciting. The labs allow kids and adults to create and play while working together and with peers. "Maker Labs" take an old-school concept and merge it with a new-school vibe; think sewing circles, knitting groups, auto shop, etc. They thus become community gathering places where people can share interests and use technology to explore and innovate. Maker labs operate under the principle of student-led inquiry rather than the older "sage on the stage" model of pedagogy.

So far, most of these labs are outside of schools, located in libraries and other settings, but some innovators are bringing them to school campuses. In traditional schools, the maker spaces often connect to STEM learning. Materials in the lab are varied, and can include electronic prototypes and kits, computers, and workshop tools such as hammers and saws. Ideally, the spaces take into account the interests of the community. For instance, at the independent school the Center for Early Education in Los Angeles, the state-of-the-art lab teaches children to work with their hands as well as their minds to see how digital concepts might translate into tangible products.

Should Phones Be Allowed in the Classroom?

Administrators must determine school policies about whether to allow students to bring their phones to school and into the classroom. On the one hand, parents who want to be able to reach their children support kids' use of phones during the school day. On the other hand, teachers must grapple with keeping their students' attention, and the distraction of an Internet-connected mobile device does not help.

Both students and teachers are torn. When surveyed, teachers overwhelmingly report that digital technologies do more to distract students than to help them academically. However, they also indicate that the Internet has a positive impact on research skills. In a 2013 study at six colleges, students reported that they used their devices nearly eleven times a day to fight boredom.[11] They also knew that they paid less attention to the teacher and said that restricting access to their devices would be beneficial to learning.

The cat is out of the bag, however. Mobile technology is already pervasive, and even though the evidence points to a cost in focus, pedagogical benefits also exist. The answer is not simple; individual teachers are the best decision makers at the classroom level.

A Pitfall: Distraction

With a smartphone in nearly every student's pocket, opportunities abound for distraction in the classroom. Nevertheless, even when phones are banned, studies find that at least half the students still manage to text. As one researcher noted, "Distraction is a big challenge but we did a couple of studies on the use of cellphones in the classroom and even when it's forbidden, 95 per cent of the students in Grade 10 and 11 were texting in class, when they're not even allowed to have a cellphone."[12] The anxiety around sneaking a text might be more distracting than using a phone openly.

An extensive research study conducted in Quebec, Canada, about the application of iPads in the classrooms asked six thousand sixth through tenth graders and their teachers how they used their new devices.[13] The good news? Even though the iPads had been at the school for just a few months, the school reported that more than 50 percent of the time they were integrated into the pedagogy. But they were used most frequently as e-books or PDF readers, and very few students availed themselves of the multimedia applications or used them to do projects. The bad news? Astonishingly, 99 percent of the students reported that the iPads distracted them, while one in three admitted to playing games.

Another study found that students who sent more texts in the classroom received lower grades in that specific class, but found no correlation between the frequency of texting, both in school and outside of the classroom, and their overall GPA. Yet another study could not find a relationship between texting frequency and GPA.[14] At this bird's-eye view, the data does not provide a clear answer for best practices.

A Promise: Classroom Participation

When I teach high school and college students, it is always immediately clear which students are nonstop talkers, which are oversharers, and which are shy and socially anxious. As an educator, I prefer to engage everyone. Classroom participation is critical as I seek to determine who needs help with the concepts. However, no matter how hard I try to draw out the more timid students, it's rare for them to speak up.

For socially anxious people who want to share their opinions, screens provide a means to do so. Not everyone will raise his hand, but that does not mean shy students do not want to be part of classroom discussion. Some forward-thinking educators use innovative means to encourage their quieter students to participate. One interesting platform, used more frequently in big lecture halls, is an audience response system (ARS), handheld devices with specialized software that links to the handheld units. During a lecture, the professor asks students questions that they can answer by pressing the corresponding button on their device.

The answers are aggregated and shown on a screen during the class. Research suggests that these systems provide valuable ways of engaging students by encouraging them to participate—moreover, this technique motivates real-time processing of the lecture.[15] Who knew that a "pop quiz" could be fun?

Some educators use the messaging application Twitter to draw shy students out. Instead of speaking up, kids can share their thoughts by tweeting from their phone or tablet. The instructor keeps his Twitter feed open and answers questions in real time. This method provides students with an outlet for expressing their views and opinions, and frequently results in participation by students who are normally intimidated by speaking up in class.[16]

The Perspective of a Teacher and Advocate for Free Media

As administrators grapple with creating school policy, individual teachers should be allowed the flexibility to decide their own classroom guidelines. Clay Shirky, an advocate for the benefits of technology, recently decided to ban laptops, tablets, and phones in his classroom. Shirky is no Luddite; he's given a TED Talk and has written for the *Harvard Business Review* and *Wired* magazine. He even teaches a college course on social media. His reasons for the technology ban, stated in an online article published in 2014, are compelling.

> The level of distraction in my classes seemed to grow, even though it was the same professor and largely the same set of topics, taught to a group of students selected using roughly the same criteria every year. The change seemed to correlate more with the rising ubiquity and utility of the devices themselves, rather than any change in me, the students, or the rest of the classroom encounter.

I've noticed that when I do have a specific reason to ask everyone to set aside their devices ("lids down," in the parlance of my department), it's as if someone has let fresh air into the room. The conversation brightens, and more recently, there is a sense of relief from many of the students. Multi-tasking is cognitively exhausting when we do it by choice, being asked to stop can come as a welcome change.[17]

Best Practices

One of our species's first technologies, the pointed stick, transformed our existence. We could have easily used the sticks to draw pictures in the dirt and never moved on. Instead, over many years, humans adapted the tool to best meet our needs and taught the next generation best practices.

Even with the best digital media content and devices, students need the guidance and support of mentors and teachers. A comprehensive summary of experimental research in the classroom found that when you compare technology-based interventions with other kinds of intervention, such as peer tutoring, technology alone is not as effective.[18] Both types of programs improved learning, but in the end, humans trumped computers. Those who champion technology in the classroom often point to individualized learning, while opponents worry that the teacher will become obsolete. As stated succinctly in a recent article in the *Harvard Educational Review,* the role of the teacher shows no sign of disappearing: "With the increasing presence of technology in the classroom, the role of an effective teacher is not diminished; instead, it becomes even more indispensable."[19]

When digital media are introduced thoughtfully, the benefits are straightforward: engaged kids learning to use the tool in productive, creative, and safe ways. Teachers in the twenty-first century need time to understand our world's most current tool, so they can integrate it successfully into the subjects they teach. Technology cannot lead the way, but people can. Below are some recommendations for best practices.

Digital Literacy

Consider the enormous amount of instructional time, both inside and outside the classroom, that guides children on the many skills required to read, write, and understand text. Children consume media beginning at a very young age and therefore need similar formal instruction to properly analyze the content and the meanings embedded within the narratives. Digital literacy is a topic that addresses this need.

In order to learn to use digital media productively, children require guidance: they need to know how to be safe online, where to go for trustworthy information, how to keep on task, how to shape their digital footprint, how to avoid plagiarism, how the laws of copyright and fair use apply in the digital world, and so much more. Digital literacy teaches these kinds of lessons. Programs that incorporate this type of literacy when they introduce Internet-connected devices will be the most successful.[20]

Professional Development

In the last few decades, the educational historian and blogger Larry Cuban witnessed too many computers sitting in classrooms unused.[21] When teachers do not know how to integrate technology into their lesson plans, they continue to teach using the methods and tools they are most comfortable with: paper, pencils, and chalkboards. Thus, when teachers are asked to bring media into their classrooms, they must be supported.

Evidence supports making an investment in professional development. A well-designed experiment in the 2011 study on the MLTI program underscores the significance of sustained professional development.[22] Over the course of two years, researchers provided face-to-face and online workshops along with peer coaching to a group of math teachers, with the goal of helping them learn to use laptops in the classroom to meet their curriculum goals (this was the experimental group); another group of math teachers, who also had laptops, received no instruction (control group). The results were promising; remember, for the one-to-one program as a whole, ten years did not affect test scores. But in just two years, the test scores of students taught by the experimental group increased by 12 percent over those of students taught by the control group. Significantly, the experimental group also outperformed the control group on the statewide math test.

Once teachers feel comfortable using laptops to teach their students, they usually take advantage of introducing digital media.[23] At least one full day of training on basic features and use should be arranged, along with ongoing instruction on how to integrate media into the curriculum. If support cannot be provided, it is unlikely that computers or other devices will be used effectively, if at all.

Other Practices and Concerns

Context is important to consider when making decisions about investing in a new technology within learning environments. When the technology plan is sustainable and the infrastructure is in place, the following steps should be considered.

- Organize a committee made up of parents, teachers, and administrators to reflect on an acceptable use policy (AUP) and to get buy-in from all stakeholders.

- The AUP should be easy to read, with clear rules for students and parents. Consequences should be considered for failure to comply.
- Before spending the time and money on Internet filters, appraise goals carefully. Pitfalls of installing filters include the inability of teachers to access learning websites, the ease with which older kids establish workarounds, and time and information lost due to overfiltering.[24]
- Put measures in place to train and assure caregivers, who often fear that devices will lead to access to inappropriate content and frequent distraction from schoolwork (e.g., hands-on training and parent education nights will assure the community that a plan is in place to guide students).
- Train teachers on how to best integrate technology into their classrooms. Create a plan for continuous professional development and shared lesson plans.
- Consider including digital literacy in the curriculum so that kids learn to engage with the Internet in safe and productive ways.

Wrap-Up and Takeaways

Wrap-Up of the Research

1. The evidence indicates that one-to-one programs neither improve nor worsen academic outcomes.
2. Ongoing and consistent professional development for teachers on best practices with technological devices can improve student learning.
3. Innovative technology and media in the classroom frequently helps quieter students feel emboldened to participate.

4. Teachers and students report that tablets and Internet access distract from learning.
5. Restricting phone use in classrooms does not appear to stop texting as kids sneak the phones and texts in.

Takeaways for Parents and Educators

1. Teachers are usually the best equipped to decide acceptable use of personal technology in their classroom.
2. If your school is considering a one-to-one program, it is important that the necessary support for the teachers is in place. In addition, tech support is critical.
3. Point the school to the excellent online resources at Common Sense Educators, (https://www.commonsensemedia.org/educators) all free and unbiased. Digital citizenship lessons for kindergarten through twelfth grade can be found here, as well as resources for teachers, such as Graphite, a free service that independently rates apps and websites for learning and provides guidelines for integrating them into the classroom. Edutopia is also a top-notch resource.
4. Recommend that the school seeks buy-in from parents before making any changes. For example, survey parents on their concerns, bring them into the discussion about the acceptable use policy, and invite outside technology education experts who can speak to parents' concerns.
5. Form a partnership with your school, the administration, and the teachers to create best practices. In the virtual world, what happens at school will come home. The village needed to raise our children is now online and offline, at home and at school.

CHAPTER 9

Video Games and Learning

These are ancient dice, made out of sheep's knuckles. Right? Before we had awesome game controllers, we had sheep's knuckles. And these represent the first game equipment designed by human beings.

—Jane McGonigal, TED Talk, 2010[1]

Game playing may be part of human DNA. References to board games are found in the writings of ancient civilizations, and sporting games date back nearly as far. Theories abound as to why games endure and evolve. Some believe they satisfy our need for social bonding. Others say they bring out humankind's competitive energies.

In the modern age, the newest category of games is electronic. A Pew Research Center poll found that 97 percent of American children ages twelve to seventeen play computer, web, portable, or console games.[2] The highly lucrative video game industry brings in more than double the revenue of Hollywood movies.[3]

Despite their popularity, a majority of parents report that video games are worse for their kids than television, computers, and mobile devices.[4] In fact, when asked about their top concerns, parents said that video games have a negative effect on their children's reading, math, speaking skills, attention span, creativity, social abilities, physical activity, and sleep. I understand the concerns, because my twelve-year-old son spends hours exploring the worlds of *Minecraft* and *Civilization*, getting lost in their sandboxes. My husband and I accordingly spend hours worrying about the time he wastes.

As parents, we sometimes feel that older media such as television, movies, and books are superior to video games, but remember that these media are passive and allow little agency. Video games are interactive; some even require physical movement, and today's games provide many opportunities for social interaction. In the physical world, we learn through both observation and action; similarly, when contemplating your child's media diet, a balance of content, both passive and interactive, should be considered.

Given that video games are part of our children's lives, it is important to understand both the pluses and the minuses. As I educated myself on the facts, my family finally made peace with our son's obsession.

Early Research on Video Games

Although she is of another generation, my former doctoral advisor, Patricia Greenfield, and I have many similarities. She has two children, a daughter and son, and, like me, her children's interests inspired some of her research. Her son, like mine, loved video games, so as a research scientist, Dr. Greenfield decided to bring an objective lens to her parenting. Along with her graduate student at the time, Kaveri Subrahmanyam, she sought to determine exactly what her son might learn from the games he loved to play. Dr. Greenfield, influenced by what she witnessed, started to think outside of the box.

Before then, most studies examined content only, principally measuring the violence within games and assessing its relationship to aggressive behavior. As video game play became more popular in the eighties, some scholars began to speculate that these games could develop competencies such as hand-eye coordination. Dr. Greenfield and Dr. Subrahmanyam decided to experimentally measure the kinds of cognitive skills that could be developed through game play.

In 1994, they published a paper entitled "Effect of Video Game Practice on Spatial Skills in Girls and Boys."[5] In it, the two scientists reported that the kids in their study who played active video games improved on assessments of spatial performance. Since their landmark study, an entire field of inquiry followed. More recently, dozens of studies built on their findings and discovered similar effects.

Spatial Ability

Spatial skills: The capacity to comprehend the spatial relation among objects. Spatial ability is believed to be a unique kind of intelligence (e.g., Howard Gardner, a Harvard professor and author of *Multiple Intelligences*, identifies "visual-spatial" as one of seven learning styles). Assembling a jigsaw puzzle, reading maps, parking in a tight space, and even respecting someone's personal space in communication: these and hundreds of other everyday activities require spatial ability.

Mental rotation: The ability to mentally turn one object and compare it to another object, one that looks completely different in space, to determine whether they are the same. Mental rotation is a particularly significant subset of spatial skills. For instance, University of Michigan scientists who trained six- and eight-year-olds on mental rotation found their scores on addition and subtraction improved.[6]

Does My Kid Need Spatial Skills?

The development of world-class talent in science, technology, engineering, and mathematics (STEM) is critical to America's global leadership.

—White House Office of Science
and Technology, 2014

If you are interested in the national conversation about education, chances are you know what STEM means. The acronym, which stands for science, technology, engineering, and mathematics, is tossed into nearly any discussion that involves technology and our future workforce. The United States is in short supply of students majoring in these fields, and hiring managers must often recruit overseas candidates. As such, companies, governments, and educators care a great deal about promoting STEM education. Fundamentally, the emphasis on STEM is about jobs, with a focus on future opportunities for minorities and women, who are underrepresented in these fields.

People with superior spatial ability tend to perform better in STEM fields. Surprisingly, these skills can easily be learned.[7] An analysis funded by the National Science Foundation and the Institute of Education Sciences, which reviewed 217 papers, found that, with practice, it is relatively easy to improve one's spatial skills. The authors of this extensive investigation also reported that training in one medium, such as video games, leads to learning that can be transferred to other spatial tasks.

Spatial skills are useful for subjects in school and for future careers. Given these facts, it behooves you as a parent to help your child improve in these skills. If you do, at the very least, your job teaching them to drive will be much easier.

Bottom Line: Spatial skills can help your child academically and in many careers.

The Benefits of Playing Video Games

While parents are anxiety ridden, schools headed by leaders in educational technology promote teaching through gaming, and, even more surprisingly, specifically video gaming. Why do some educators believe so fervently in the favorable impact of video games, while many parents not only feel these games are a waste of time but also that they adversely affect children's health? As noted earlier, a critical reason that many teachers promote learning through gaming is that video and computer games have been proven over and over again to help kids develop cognitive skills that help them perform better in math and science.

Others imagine using motivational game mechanics and applying them to academic learning. This is not a new concept; some people call it putting chocolate on broccoli. However, in the past, when educational games were introduced in a learning setting they could not hold a child's interest. Precocious kids quickly recognized that the games were designed to teach rather than entertain, and became bored. The games of the twenty-first century, however, with their rich graphics, social interactivity, and complicated game play, represent an entirely new way to teach and intrigue students.[8] This is one reason so many academics, educators, and marketers, seek to explore the mechanisms involved.

Moreover, extensive research underscores the benefits of all kinds of video gaming, even those that are intended primarily for consumer entertainment. The evidence is so overwhelming that, in 2013, *American Psychologist*, a top journal in the field of psychology, published an article summarizing the positive research entitled "The Benefits of Playing Video Games."[9] In this article, scientists summarized much of the exciting new research on the benefits of electronic gaming, which we'll explore below.

Cognitive Benefits

Most parents, including me, will find this nearly impossible to believe, but evidence from neuroscience and cognitive psychology suggests that first-person shooter games positively impact cognitive abilities. In study after study, attentional control and spatial skills were found to improve in groups that play action games.[10] These findings persist and have been replicated many times. Moreover, the learning is not isolated to the laboratory and transfers to other contexts.

A well-established finding is that laparoscopic surgeons who play video games improve their accuracy in the operating room. These are the doctors who operate while looking at a screen hooked up to a tiny video camera inserted in their patient's body. In a study published in 2013, researchers randomly assigned forty-two postgraduate residents in surgery to one of two groups; one group played on the Nintendo Wii for four weeks and one did not.[11] Before and after the intervention, each group of the medical students took tests on a variety of tasks in the laparoscopic simulator. In session one, held before the training, no differences existed between the two groups; but by session two, in test after test, the Wii group performed significantly better than the control group; in one task the difference in accuracy between the two groups was 73 percent! Importantly, the Wii games in the study with surgeons were rated E for everyone.

Real-world and highly technical skills that improve from increased video game playing may not be information you want to share with your kids, but perhaps consider this line of research before you ban all games. And certainly before you or your loved ones goes under the knife.

Other thinking skills that could develop through game play include problem solving and enhanced creativity. One study found that first-person shooter games are associated with an ability to flexibly update information.[12] However, these kinds of games are frequently violent and labeled for mature audiences only; naturally, their benefits must be weighed against the aggressive and graphic imagery (more on this later in chapter).

Motivational Benefits

Imagine your child tackling his homework with the same enthusiasm he displays for video games. I was skeptical that a computer game could provide any academic knowledge, until my son started sharing with me random facts about the universe. Literally, the universe. He didn't learn this information in school or from my husband or me; he learned it from a computer game! He was so dedicated to the topic that he astounded a former NASA engineer with his encyclopedic knowledge of the space missions. When he was younger, he memorized the entire history of basketball because he played the NBA series of video games distributed by Electronic Arts.

Incremental goals, intermittent rewards, and immediate feedback are all elements, proven to motivate, found in video games. These findings lend support to the game enthusiasts who believe that game-based learning can replace the traditional classroom.

Emotional Benefits

The authors of the *American Psychologist* article speculated that kids could also practice and develop emotion-regulation skills through gaming. Games do seem to provide an outlet for processing emotions. Several years ago, I attended a lecture by a former Harvard scientist who spent years speaking to children about video games.[13] She found that kids used gaming as a means of dealing with their negative emotions. She made the valid point that game play was a better coping mechanism than substance abuse. Supporting her observation, research found that video game players smoke less marijuana than non-players.[14]

We all need to zone out sometimes. After a stressful day at school, my son plays video games; watching *Parenthood* and *Scandal* in the evening is my old-school way of coping with a stressful day.

Other Health Benefits

Games not only impact emotional and cognitive behaviors, they can also positively impact mental health treatments. For instance, video games and online gaming are used in therapeutic interventions that help with ADHD, anxiety, and autism.[15] Indeed, their use is so effective that a peer-reviewed journal called *Games for Health,* dedicated to how game technology can be used to improve physical and mental health and well-being, publishes papers on a bimonthly basis.

> **Bottom Line:** Don't despair if your child loves to play video games. Numerous benefits exist.

No Longer a Loner

Are gamers in the twenty-first century socially isolated children who try to avoid human interaction? Evidence indicates otherwise. Sixty-two percent of gamers report that they play their video games with others, either in person or online.[16] Community engagement is highlighted by an intriguing phenomenon, facilitated by the growth of YouTube, the rise of the video game channels.

For instance, a handsome Swedish YouTuber who calls himself PewDiePie claims the top channel on YouTube, with more than thirty million subscribers. If you have never heard of this person, perhaps it is because PewDiePie doesn't do anything resembling traditional entertainment; he does not play music or perform skits. Instead, he provides real-time gaming commentary, videotaping his game play and sharing his enjoyment and reactions to the game with his online audience.

This idea of watching a video of someone playing a video game seems absurd to me and to other adults I've spoken with; I've tried watching with my son, but it is like watching paint dry. Yet channels like PewDiePie's are among the most popular on YouTube. PewDiePie swears, laughs, and makes fun of the game; he feels like a cool older brother, and the kids who watch his channel get to bask in his aura. The comments, which can number in the thousands, allow gamers to share their points of view and participate.

These channels are the modern-day equivalent of kids gathered around the pinball wizard playing at an arcade game. It's a testament to the human need to be social; thanks to the Internet and video-sharing platforms, those children who enjoy game play can always find someone else who feels similarly, even when they are sitting at home in their pajamas.

Are All Games Equal?

Games are a big business, not only for kids but also for adults. In 2014, a broad spectrum of electronic games was popular for people ages eight to eighty.[17] My own kids are enthusiastic consumers: my daughter is presently infatuated with a game called *Cut the Rope,* which she plays on her phone; my son plays a computer-based game called *Kerbal Space Program.* Even though I currently am not interested in gaming, when I was in seventh grade, I played *Pac-Man* obsessively on a small handheld device. Perhaps that explains my strong grades in calculus in high school, and sadly, since I now refuse to play electronic games, my declining ability to understand my daughter's math homework.

Gamers come in all shapes and sizes. In fact, the average American gamer is a thirty-one-year-old woman who plays primarily social and casual games such as *Words with Friends*. Electronic game titles are also varied. Top-selling video games range from mature action games such as *Call of Duty* to sports games for everyone such as *Madden NFL*. Some of the most popular computer games are simulation franchises like *The Sims* and strategy series like *StarCraft*.

Of course, not all content is equal. Exceedingly graphic violent video games, with their realistic portraits of aggression, are particularly unpleasant. Thankfully, hundreds of new games are published every year, and while a few especially violent video games grab the headlines, many critically acclaimed titles provide excellent alternatives.

The Variety of Games and Gamers

A wide variety of content exists, with titles that appeal to many different tastes and interests. The Entertainment Software Association separates sales of games into video game and computer game lists, and games played on mobile applications make up another category entirely. Below are some titles of great games in each category that Common Sense Media rates highly for entertainment and learning.

Video games: *Minecraft, Madden NFL 25, Disney Infinity, Skylanders Swap Force*

Computer games: *StarCraft, Minecraft, Sim City, The Sims*

Mobile games: *Candy Crush Saga, Farm Heroes Saga, Angry Birds*

> **Bottom Line:** Pay attention to the content of digital games. Plenty of high-quality titles are available.

Video Games—The Answer to Failures in Education?

Given all the evidence that games teach important mental skills, it seems natural that some educators, and gaming enthusiasts, would suggest that video gaming could transform learning. In fact, a cottage industry has grown up around this topic. For example, an organization called Games, Learning, and Society holds an annual academic conference, conducts research, teaches classes, and develops products, all with the goal of creating games to improve humankind.

One group of academics and educators developed a public school, optimistically called Quest to Learn, centered on using the design principles of games to teach. In 2009, this well-funded middle school, supported by grants from the MacArthur Foundation and other generous donors, opened its doors in New York City. Expectations were high; the *New York Times* published an enthusiastic article about the school called "Learning by Playing: Video Games in the Classroom." However, five years later, the evidence that the curriculum works is sparse. The website GreatSchools.org, which aggregates parent reviews of most schools in the United States on a ten-point scale, reports a rating of six. Other data indicate that, even with tremendous resources and support, the test scores of kids attending the school are just average. Certainly, the possibilities are intriguing, but kids, not to mention teachers, learn in many different ways, which means the opportunity to scale (i.e., to grow rapidly and efficiently) is limited. Even if your child seems destined to become a game designer, I would not enroll her in this sort of school just yet.

> **Bottom Line:** Video games are not the answer to problems in our educational system.

The Costs of Playing Video Games

While video games do have benefits, the costs can be serious and must be considered. Parents are worried. The two concerns that receive the most attention are violence in video games and addiction to game play.

Violent Video Games

From Columbine to Newtown, when a violent rampage erupts at a school, video games are usually brought up as a possible causal factor in the shooter's actions. It is extremely difficult, however, to definitively answer the question of whether antisocial people are drawn to aggressive video games, which could then spur their natural tendencies, or if these games *cause* a child to play out the portrayed violent scenarios. In other words, which came first, the chicken or the egg? The sad reality is that the numerous reasons for these kinds of tragic events are nuanced and difficult to pinpoint.

Two psychological research camps dominate the national conversation about whether violent video games lead to aggressive behavior. The first, led by Craig Anderson from Iowa State University, offers ample evidence that violent video games have negative effects.[18] The second, led by Christopher Ferguson from Stetson University, provides proof that violent video games do not lead to aggressive behavior.[19] Each of these research groups continues to duke it out in the academic literature. While it is clear that both these scientists believe passionately in their theories, what confounds their debate is that both labs look at some of the same studies. Evidently, the argument is not yet settled.

Recently, I read convincing new evidence that violent video game play does *not* cause aggressive behavior in a peer-reviewed article entitled "Causal or Spurious: Using Propensity Score Matching to Detangle the Relationship Between Violent Video Games and Violent Behavior."[20] The authors of the paper, faculty at university departments of sociology and criminal justice, utilized a newer method of analysis, called propensity scoring, to equalize the many different factors that explain individual behavior. Scientists who use propensity scores match participants on as many variables as possible; for example, in this paper the authors investigated what kind of video games participants played, as well as variables such as gender, previous antisocial behavior, etc.—all told, 150 factors were considered. Then matched pairs were created. For example, two boys who went to the same school, had parents of the same ethnicity and socioeconomic status, held similar GPA averages, and accessed identical digital media in the home were compared (these were just a few of the many, many variables participants were matched on). The only difference between the two was that one boy played violent video games and the other did not.

In total, the researchers reviewed and matched data on 6,567 eighth-grade kids. They first reported correlational findings between the two variables of interest: those who played violent video games and exhibited deviant behavior. As in many other published reports, they found a strong positive relationship between the two. However, relying on correlational data to answer scientific questions can produce misleading results. For example, an inverse relationship exists between the sale of video games, which grew rapidly, and rates of violent juvenile crime, which decreased. If you relied on this correlational data, you might give video games the credit for the drop in criminality.

Using the propensity score analysis, scientists were able to dig deeper into their research subject to attempt to untangle the most important question; as the title of their paper suggests, is the relationship causal or spurious?

They found no significant relationship between boys who played violent video games and either aggressive or nonaggressive behavior. In fact, the only significant relationship they found was one that was negative—for marijuana. Boys who played violent video games smoked less pot than those who did not. However, they did find that for the one-third of girls in the sample who reported playing violent video games, 12 percent of those girls were more likely to exhibit aggressive behavior.

This study provides compelling, and hopefully reassuring, evidence that these games should not change the behavior of the vast majority of children, particularly boys. The authors conclude by saying that they found little support for the assumptions of policy makers and popular media reports that violent media are linked to antisocial conduct. However, if your child plays these kinds of games and exhibits unusually angry behavior afterward, it would be wise to limit use. More importantly, seek help from a mental health professional.

> Bottom Line: Violent video games do not appear to *cause* deviant behavior.

Addiction

My son and almost all of his friends are "infected." They all share similar personality traits which parallel those in drug addicts. They lie and steal to further their addiction. My son has been banned from any and all video gaming due to such incidents. He has subsequently returned to the son we used to know.... While they may be enhancing their hand-eye coordination, they are missing out on many more important aspects of life. What a shame.

—User comment on GreatSchools.org article, 2014

The comment above was written in response to a published article about some of the research on video games.[21] It is indeed true that some children can become addicted to game play. In the U.S., the prevalence rate is reported to be anywhere from 3 to 11 percent. True addiction is a serious affliction, and it is important to carefully consider your child's behavior before making an assumption. If you suspect your child may be addicted, please look at page 73 and ask yourself, and your child, the questions listed there.

Girls and Video Games

One of the things that I really strongly believe in is that we need to have more girls interested in math, science, and engineering. We've got half the population that is way underrepresented in those fields and that means that we've got a whole bunch of talent...not being encouraged the way they need to.

—President Barack Obama, February 2013

In a 2005 lecture at the National Bureau of Economic Research (NBER) Conference on Diversifying the Science & Engineering Workforce, Lawrence Summers, then president of Harvard, made a statement that created a furor. He shared with the audience some of the reasons that fewer women were in mathematic and scientific fields, and pointed to genetic differences between the sexes. Here is what he said in that speech:

It does appear that on many, many different human attributes—height, weight, propensity for criminality, overall

IQ, mathematical ability, scientific ability—there is relatively clear evidence that whatever the difference in means—which can be debated—there is a difference in the standard deviation, and variability of a male and a female population.

The outcry to this statement was loud and definitive, and Dr. Summers ended up resigning his post. Yet the most prestigious math accomplishment in the world, the Fields Medal, established in 1936, was awarded to just one woman in its entire history. Sexism or lack of ability? Did Dr. Summers have a point?

It is well known in academic fields that males outperform females in spatial abilities. And if spatial abilities are important for STEM achievement, perhaps women are not as capable as men in math, science, and engineering. However, studies on spatial skills and video games point to socialization, or at the very least the choice of leisure pursuits, as one potential reason girls perform worse on tests of these capabilities.[22]

The 1994 study by Dr. Greenfield and Dr. Subrahmanyam, which tested whether spatial skills could be learned through video gaming, measured the differences between the ten-year-old female and male participants.[23] Before the experiment, the girls performed significantly worse than the boys on a test of their spatial skills. Moreover, most of the boys spent more time than the girls playing video games.

During the experiment, each kid was assigned to play one of two games, *Marble Madness* (an action video game with spatial elements) or *Conjecture* (a computerized word game with no spatial component built into the game play); the kids played three times for forty-five minutes per session over a window of a few weeks. Then, the subjects came back and were tested again. As expected, the children who played *Marble Madness* performed better on the test of spatial skills than those who played *Conjecture*.

Unexpectedly, Subrahmanyam and Greenfield did not find an

effect of gender (i.e., that girls improved more than boys in spatial ability). They reran the test and made a fascinating finding; the children with low spatial abilities to begin with, a mix of boys and girls, were the ones who improved significantly after playing *Marble Madness*. Spatial skills can be developed by video game play, and girls tend to play fewer video games, thus their baseline skills were much lower than those of the boys.

The conclusion of their paper, written more than twenty years ago was: "With computers fast becoming the dominant technology of the day, video games may serve as an informal technique for equipping girls and women with the skills and motivation to ensure they are not left behind in the future." Despite their insight, in 2015, fewer women major in computer science than ever before; in 1985 over 35 percent of people who majored in computer science were women, today, the number has dropped to under 20 percent.[24]

Fourteen years later, another group of scientists out of the University of Toronto conducted a remarkably similar experiment, with notable results.[25] In their study they asked college students to play *Medal of Honor: Pacific Assault*, a 3-D first-person shooting game, for ten hours. Females, who scored lower than males on the pretest, improved more than males on the post. Again, the mere experience of playing video games nearly eliminated the preexisting gender difference in spatial cognition.

> **Bottom Line:** Encourage your girls to play video games, especially ones with a spatial component.

Conclusion

Video games develop skills that support academic learning and workforce training. Even first-person shooter video games develop STEM skills, the kinds of skills that CEOs like Eric Schmidt of Google say are sorely lacking in our workforce. Children in the twenty-first century need this kind of scientific and technological literacy. With so many engaging, interactive, and social games available, there is fantastic content that our kids can both enjoy and learn from. It is high time that the fears that parents hold about video game play are reconsidered.

Wrap-Up and Takeaways

Wrap-Up of the Research

1. Video games develop spatial skills.
2. Spatial skills are easily learned and contribute to success in STEM fields.
3. Because young girls typically do not play video games, socialization may be one reason that girls do not test as strongly in spatial skills. Girls who play video games with a spatial component improve dramatically in this arena.
4. Playing video games improves the accuracy of laparoscopic surgeons.
5. The evidence that violent video games *cause* violent behavior is not conclusive.

Takeaways for Parents

1. Some video game play is perfectly fine for your child.
2. Balance your child's video game play with other activities; while kids can learn some useful skills, and the games can be social, kids need balance and face-to-face time.
3. Consider the content carefully. While evidence suggests that even "violent" video games teach cognitive skills and are

unlikely to lead your child to be aggressive, they include many other potentially offensive characteristics such as misogyny and crime-glorifying behavior.

4. Know your child; if you see problem behavior, unusual conduct, or signs of addiction, seek help from a mental health professional.

EPILOGUE

Art challenges technology, and technology inspires art.

—John Lasseter, Pixar cofounder

Storytellers in the business of imagining futuristic scenarios are frequently influenced by the technological marvels of their day. For example, Stanley Kubrick's *2001*, made during the excitement of the lunar landing, imagined a future in which humans travelled through space to outposts on other planets. In *Blade Runner*, filmed in 1982 as computers started to enter the mainstream, Ridley Scott created a bleak future filled with artificially intelligent machines.

Our technological marvel is the Internet and mobile technology. A cult English anthology television series called *Black Mirror* takes a thought-provoking look at the consequences of these modern affordances. Since many of the episodes are set in the "present" with ordinary citizens, they ring both ominous and real. For example, in one episode the majority of the citizens install cameras behind their ears to film every second of every day. When a young married professional becomes consumed with the idea that his wife is having an affair, his ability to access real footage in the lives of those involved leads to an unhealthy obsession. The story thus smartly asks the question, do we really want to document every moment of our lives?

We cannot turn back, nor should we want to. But we can teach young people, who have not experienced otherwise, to consider unanticipated costs. Two critical issues are loss of privacy and the potential that mediated communication will replace face-to-face time, and parents and educators can focus on guiding youth in these areas. Teens hate it when parents "spy"; accordingly, the concept of privacy is salient. And since kids crave time with their friends, and in fact prefer to be with them face to face, help them recognize what they give up when they focus on mediated communications. Our role is to shape societal norms; it's an ambitious but feasible project, and it's how cultures evolve. The change starts with each one of us.

Privacy

The CEO of the national nonprofit Common Sense Media, James P. Steyer, is a passionate advocate for kids. When I started working with this organization in 2011, we threw an event in Los Angeles that centered on the importance of protecting children's privacy in the digital age. Jim argued that Silicon Valley does not adequately consider privacy when creating new products and platforms. He explained that technology moves fast, government is slow, and parents must lead the way in teaching their children what they give up when their activities are tracked online.

Back then I had not considered the topic carefully. However, in the years since, our loss of privacy in the twenty-first century became all too real. From Edward Snowden's NSA leaks to the hackers who released Sony data around the release of the film *The Interview,* current events demonstrate that the stakes become higher each day.

The classic Francis Ford Coppola film *The Conversation,* starring Gene Hackman, explored surveillance in the seventies. In the film, Hackman's character ends up paranoid and seemingly crazy; he frantically rips up the floors in his apartment because he believes that he is being watched. Viewed today, the film seems prescient of the new millennium.

Reflect on some of the statistics below, and share them with your children; ask them to consider the pluses and minuses:

- At the 2015 Consumer Electronic Show the theme was "The Internet of Things," featuring everyday household items with Internet connectivity. Some of the exciting new products included a connected toothbrush, Internet-enabled door locks, and stoves that text (seriously).
- Wearable tech and household items that connect to the Internet mean that companies, and hackers, will be able to track our daily practices.
- More than one-third of U.S. parents with children under two posted their sonograms online.[1]
- *Consumer Reports* estimated that 4.8 million people have used Facebook to say where they planned to go on a certain day. Another 4.7 million have liked a Facebook page about health conditions or treatments. Thirteen million said they had never set or did not know about Facebook's privacy tools, and 28 percent of users shared wall posts beyond friends.[2]
- In 2011, in the U.S. and Canada, Facebook made $9.51 per user.[3]

I personally don't believe holding businesses accountable will change their practices. Companies are driven by profit, and advertising is the preferred means to increase revenue. Big data is big business. Companies collect our information and save it. However, we willingly share that information in the virtual world, where they can legally access it. As such, I agree with Google vice president and chief Internet evangelist Vint Cerf, who said that rather than relying on regulations, people will have "to develop social conventions that are more respectful of people's privacy."[4]

The topic of privacy is complex, with many stakeholders, and some people argue that kids do not care.[5] This may be true, but our role, as always, is to help guide youth to think about their future.

Human Connection

In the 2013 masterpiece *Her*, Spike Jonze envisioned a future in which humans interact with artificial intelligence (AI); unlike in *Blade Runner*, the AI in this film was not embodied. No robots; instead, voices emanate from operating systems (OS). The lead character, Theodore, a lonely divorcé played by Joaquin Phoenix, falls in love with his brand new OS, named Samantha (voice played by Scarlett Johansson). Samantha, able to transcend time and space, and without the encumbrance of a body, eventually leaves Theodore to explore other planes of being. While the premise is unsettling, the end is hopeful. Theodore sits with a good friend, a human, who puts her head on his shoulder.

Black Mirror also explored falling in love with artificial intelligence. In the episode entitled "Be Right Back," when Martha's husband Ash dies, his online presence lives on. Martha orders an embodied version of her husband, with a hard drive filled with his "personality" lifted from his own online postings. At first, she is thrilled to reunite with her husband, even if he is not exactly the same. The novelty soon wears off, and it becomes clear that while the synthetic Ash is perfectly enjoyable, he lacks depth and intellectual complexity. In the final scene, Ash is hidden in the attic, a mere "toy" Martha's daughter plays with.

These thoughtful stories illustrate beautifully the human desire for true connection with other human beings. While computers, and even AI, might satisfy some of our needs, our minds, bodies, and souls crave in-person relationships. As I wrote in chapter 4, parents must teach children the importance of face-to-face time. Creating a home environment that reflects these basic and enduring human values is a crucial role of modern parents.

The mythologist Joseph Campbell wrote that stories help us make sense of our lives. As a former movie executive who is married to a screenwriter, I believe fervently in the power of fiction. Although 2001 came and went, and we are no closer to the future that Stanley Kubrick imagined, the themes in his film still resonate and inform the movies, TV shows, and even video games of today. In the twenty-first century, technological innovations develop at an exponential rate, and the potential for the transformation of human existence is unsettling. The imagination of talented storytellers in the business of envisioning the future is often scarily on target. Perhaps we can learn from their imaginations as well as from science.

NOTES

Introduction

1. M.E. Schmidt and E.A. Vandewater, "Media and Attention, Cognition and School Achievement," in *Children and Electronic Media*, vol. 18, Future of Children 1 (Princeton, NJ: Brookings Institute, 2008), 77.
2. V.J. Rideout, U.G. Foehr, and D.F. Roberts, *Generation M2: Media in the Lives of 8-18 Year-Olds* (Menlo Park, CA: Kaiser Family Foundation, 2010).
3. Stephanie Mlot, "Smartphone Adoption Rate Fastest in Tech History," *PC Magazine*, August 27, 2012, http://www.pcmag.com/article2/0,2817,2408960,00.asp.
4. "Internet Growth Statistics," *Internet World Stats*, 2014, http://www.internetworld stats.com.
5. NPD Group, "Internet Connected Devices Surpass Half a Billion in U.S. Homes, According to The NPD Group," March 18, 2013, https://www.npd .com/wps/portal/npd/us/news/press-releases/internet-connected-devices -surpass-half-a-billion-in-u-s-homes-according-to-the-npd-group/.
6. Common Sense Media, "Zero to Eight: Children's Media Use in America," October 28, 2013, http://www.commonsensemedia.org/research/ zero-to-eight-childrens-media-use-in-america-2013.
7. Karl Fisch, and modified by Scott McLeod, *Did You Know: Best of Shift Happens*, 2010, https://www.youtube.com/watch?v=jp_oyHY5bug.
8. Ibid.

Chapter 1

1. Elizabeth Gilbert, "In Defense of Teenagers," Facebook post, January 22, 2015.
2. Entertainment Software Association, *Essential Facts About the Computer and Video Game Industry*, 2014.
3. J. Mazel, "The 50 Best Selling Video Games of the 1990s Worldwide," 2009, http://www.vgchartz.com/article/4145/the-50-best-selling-videogames-of -the-1990s-worldwide/.

4. APA, *Report of the APA Task Force on the Sexualization of Girls* (APA, 2010).

5. K.M Thompson and F. Yokata, "Violence, Sex and Profanity in Films: Correlation of Movie Ratings with Content," *Medscape General Medicine* 6 (2004).

6. C. Sabina, J. Wolak, and D. Finkelhor, "The Nature and Dynamics of Internet Pornography Exposure for Youth," *Cyberpsychology and Behavior* 11 (2008).

7. L.D. Johnston et al., *Monitoring the Future: National Survey Results on Drug Use, 1975–2013* (University of Michigan: National Institute on Drug Abuse at the National Institutes of Health, 2013).

8. *Trends in the Prevalence of Sexual Behaviors and HIV Testing, 1991–2013* (CDC, 2014), http://www.cdc.gov/healthyyouth/yrbs/pdf/trends/us_sexual_trend _yrbs.pdf.

9. *Youth Violence: National Statistics* (CDC, 2013), http://www.cdc.gov/violence prevention/youthviolence/stats_at-a_glance/vca_temp-trends.html.

10. FBI, "Uniform Crime Report," 2014, http://www.fbi.gov/about-us/cjis/ ucr/ucr-publications#Hate.

11. J. McCarthy, "Same-Sex Marriage Support Reaches New High at 55%," Gallup (May 2014), http://www.gallup.com/poll/169640/sex-marriage -support-reaches-new-high.aspx.

12. "CNN/ORC Poll," 2012, http://i2.cdn.turner.com/cnn/2012/images/04/ 16/rel4b.pdf.

13. M. Prensky, "Digital Natives, Digital Immigrants," *On the Horizon* 9, no. 1 (2001): 1–6.

14. L. Plowman and J. McPake, "Seven Myths About Young Children and Technology," *Childhood Education*, February 2013.

15. Entertainment Software Association, *Essential Facts About the Computer and Video Game Industry*, 2014.

16. Havas Worldwide, "The New Dynamics of Family," 2015, http://www .slideshare.net/HavasWorldwide/the-new-dynamics-of-family.

17. M. Madden et al., *Teens and Technology 2013*, Pew Internet and American Life Project (Washington, DC: Pew Research Center).

18. D. Quinn, L. Chen, and M. Mulvenna, "Does Age Make a Difference in the Behavior of Online Social Network Users?," IEEE International Conferences on Internet of Things, and Cyber, Political and Social Computing, 2011.

19. "Broadband Technology Fact Sheet," Pew Research Center, 2014, http:// www.pewinternet.org/fact-sheets/broadband-technology-fact-sheet/.

20. C. Steiner-Adair, *The Big Disconnect: Protecting Childhood and Family Relationships in the Digital Age* (New York: HarperCollins, 2013).

21. *Parenting in the Age of Digital Technology: A National Survey* (Northwestern University: Center on Media and Human Development, 2013).

22. "Intrusive Monitoring of Internet Use by Parents Actually Leads Adolescents to Increase Their Risky Online Behavior," *Science Daily*, January 21, 2015, http://www.sciencedaily.com/releases/2015/01/150121093507.htm.
23. A. Duerager and S. Livingstone, "How Can Parents Support Children's Internet Safety?," *EU Kids Online*, February 2012, http://eprints.lse.ac.uk/42872/1/How%20can%20parents%20support%20children's%20internet%20safety(lsero).pdf.
24. J.J. Davies and D.A. Gentile, "Responses to Children's Media Use in Families with and without Siblings: A Family Development Perspective," *Family Relations* 61 (2012).
25. Havas Worldwide, "The New Dynamics of Family."

Chapter 2

1. M. Gentzkow and J.M. Shapiro, "Preschool Television Viewing and Adolescent Test Scores: Historical Evidence from the Coleman Study," *The Quarterly Journal of Economics* (2008).
2. Policy Statement, *Children, Adolescents, and the Media* (American Academy of Pediatrics, 2013).
3. A. Bandura, D. Ross, and S. Ross, "Transmission of Aggression Through Imitation of Aggressive Models," *Journal of Abnormal and Social Psychology* 63 (1961).
4. J. Watson, *Behaviorism* (New Brunswick, NJ: The People's Institute Publishing Company, 1924).
5. O. Pascalis, M. de Haan, and C.A. Nelson, "Is Face Processing Species-Specific During the First Year of Life?," *Science* 296 (2002).
6. C. Moore and P.J. Dunham, eds., *Joint Attention: Its Origins and Role in Development* (Erlbaum, 1995).
7. M.B. Robb, R.A. Richert, and E. Wartella, "Just a Talking Book? Word Learning from Watching Baby Videos," *British Journal of Developmental Psychology* 27 (2009): 27–45.
8. F.J. Zimmerman, D. A. Christakis, and A.N. Meltzoff, "Associations Between Media Viewing and Language Development in Children Under Age 2 Years," *The Journal of Pediatrics* 151 (2007).
9. Robb, Richert, and Wartella, "Just a Talking Book?"
10. P.K. Kuhl, F.M. Tsao, and H.M. Liu, "Foreign-Language Experience in Infancy: Effects of Short-Term Exposure and Social Interaction on Phonetic Learning," *Proceedings of the National Academy of Science* 100 (2003): 9096–9101.
11. L. Guernsey, *Screentime: How Electronic Media—from Baby Videos to Educational Software—Affects Your Child* (New York: Basic Books, 2011).

12. G.L. Troseth and J.S. DeLoache, "The Medium Can Obscure the Message: Young Children's Understanding of Video," *Child* 69 (1998): 950–65.

13. H. Hayne, J. Herbert, and G. Simcock, "Imitation from Television by 24- and 30-Month-Olds," *Developmental Science* 6 (2003): 254–61.

14. A.R. Lauricella et al., "Contingent Computer Interactions for Young Children's Object Retrieval Success," *Journal of Applied Developmental Psychology* 31 (2010): 362–69.

15. G.A. Strouse and G.L. Troseth, "Supporting Toddlers' Transfer of Word Learning from Video," *Cognitive Development* 30 (2014).

16. S. Roseberry et al., "Live Action: Can Young Children Learn Verbs from Video?," *Child Development* 80 (2009).

17. S. Roseberry, K. Hirch-Pasek, and R.M. Golinkoff, "Skype Me! Socially Contingent Interactions Help Toddlers Learn Language," *Child Development* 85 (2014).

18. Davies and Gentile, "Responses to Children's Media Use in Families with and without Siblings: A Family Development Perspective."

19. M.E. Schmidt et al., "Television Viewing in Infancy and Child Cognition at 3 Years of Age in a US Cohort," *Pediatrics* 123 (2009).

Chapter 3

1. Gary Turk, "Look Up, " YouTube video, posted by Gary Turk, April 25, 2014, https://www.youtube.com/watch?v=Z7dLU6fk9QY.

2. Common Sense Media, *Social Media, Social Life: How Teens View Their Digital Lives* (Common Sense Media, 2012).

3. JWT Intelligence, "Gen Z: Digital in Their DNA," April 2012, http://www.jwtintelligence.com/wp-content/uploads/2012/04/F_INTERNAL_Gen_Z_0418122.pdf .

4. Cisco, "Cisco Visual Networking Index: Global Mobile Data Traffic Forecast Update 2014–2019 White Paper," February 2015, http://www.cisco.com/c/en/us/solutions/collateral/service-provider/visual-networking-index-vni/white_paper_c11-520862.html.

5. Karl Fisch, and modified by Scott McLeod, *Did You Know: Best of Shift Happens.*"

6. E. Limer, "The First Text Message Was Sent 20 Years Ago Today," *Gizmodo*, December 3, 2012, http://gizmodo.com/5965121/the-first-text-message-was-sent-20-years-ago-today.

7. Cisco, "Cisco Visual Networking Index: Global Mobile Data Traffic Forecast Update 2014–2019 White Paper."

8. Kukil Bora, "Mobile App Store Annual Downloads to Reach 102 Billion in 2013; IOS, Android Stores to Account for 90% of Downloads by 2017,"

International Business Times, September 19, 2013, http://www.ibtimes.com/ mobile-app-store-annual-downloads-reach-102-billion-2013-ios-android -stores-account-90-downloads.

9. M.A. Harrison and A.L. Gilmore, "U Txt WHEN? College Students' Social Contexts of Text Messaging," *The Social Science Journal* 49 (2012).

10. JWT Intelligence, "Gen Z: Digital in Their DNA," April 2012, http:// www.jwtintelligence.com/wpcontent/uploads/2012/04/F_INTERNAL _Gen_Z_0418122.pdf.

11. Ibid.

12. N.B. Ellison, C. Steinfeld, and C. Lampe, "Connection Strategies: Social Capital Implications of Facebook-Enabled Communication Practices," *New Media & Society*, (2010) 1–20.

13. D. Quinn, L. Chen, and M. Mulvenna, "Does Age Make a Difference in the Behavior of Online Social Network Users?," IEEE International Conferences on Internet of Things, and Cyber, Political and Social Computing, 2011.

14. C.D. Firth and U. Firth, "Mechanisms of Social Cognition," *Annual Review of Psychology* 63 (2012): 287–313.

15. S.J. Blakemore, "How Does the Brain Deal with the Social World?," *Neuro Report* 14 (2003): 1–10.

16. L. Sproull and S. Kiesler, "Reducing Social Context Cues: Electronic Mail in Organizational Communication," *Management Science* 32, no. 11 (1988): 1492–1512.

17. "Paul Ekman Group, Training," 2015, http://www.paulekman.com/products/.

18. C. Izard et al., "Emotion Knowledge as a Predictor of Social Behavior and Academic Competence in Children at Risk," *Psychological Science* 12 (2001): 352.

19. M.L. Knapp and J.A. Hall, *Nonverbal Communication in Human Interaction*, 7th ed. (Boston, MA: Wadsworth Cengage Learning, 2010).

20. Ibid.

21. Erdley and Asher, "A Social Goals Perspective on Children's Social Competence," *Journal of Emotional and Behavioral Disorders* 7, no. 156 (1999): 156–68.

22. J.R. Brown and J. Dunn, "Continuities in Emotion Understanding from Three to Six Years," *Child Development* 67 (1996): 789–802.

23. Sproull and Kiesler, "Reducing Social Context Cues: Electronic Mail in Organizational Communication."

24. Y.T. Uhls, "What Happens When Kids Go Cold Turkey from Their Screens for 5 Days?," 2014, http://www.huffingtonpost.com/yalda-t-uhls/what-happens -when-kids-go-cold-turkey-from-their-screens-for-5-days_b_5700805 .html.

25. Y.T. Uhls et al., "Five Days at Outdoor Education Camp Without Screens Improves Preteen Skills with Nonverbal Emotion Cues," *Computers in Human Behavior*, (2014).

26. S. Nowicki, Jr., "Manual for the Receptive Tests of the DANVA2," 2010.

27. J. Magill-Evans et al., "The Child and Adolescent Social Perception Measure," *Journal of Nonverbal Behavior* 19 (1995): 151.

28. J. Magill-Evans, K. Manyk, and A. Cameron-Sadava, "Child and Adolescent Social Perception Measure: Manual" (Unpublished manuscript, 1995).

29. J. Radesky et al., "Patterns of Mobile Device Use by Caregivers and Children During Meals in a Fast Food Restaurants," *Pediatrics*, (2014).

30. J. Radesky et al., "Maternal Mobile Device Use During a Structured Parent–Child Interaction Task," *Academic Pediatrics*, (2014).

31. C. Palsson, "That Smarts! Smartphones and Child Injuries" (Department of Economics, Yale, 2014).

32. *Highlights* magazine, *The State of the Kid 2014*, Highlights for Children, 2014, https://cdn.highlights.com/hfc/highlights/state-of-the-kid/Highlights -SOTK14.pdf?_ga=1.157347514.1483083552.1403891518.

33. Michele Borba, "Parents Too Plugged In? That's What Our Kids Say," *Pediatric Safety*, 2012, http://www.pediatricsafety.net/index.php?s=She%E2%80% 99s%20always%20on%20her%20blackberry.%20It%E2%80%99s%20 soooo%20annoying.

34. Growing Wireless, "Kids Wireless Use Quick Facts," 2015, http://www .growingwireless.com/get-the-facts/quick-facts.

35. L. Sakari et al., "Adolescents' Electronic Media Use at Night, Sleep Disturbance, and Depressive Symptoms in the Smartphone Age," *Journal of Youth and Adolescence* 44 (2014).

36. R.S. Weisskirch, "Parenting by Cell Phone: Parental Monitoring of Adolescents and Family Relations," *Journal of Youth Adolescence* 38 (2009).

37. "Intrusive Monitoring of Internet Use by Parents Actually Leads Adolescents to Increase Their Risky Online Behavior," *Science Daily*, January 21, 2015, http://www.sciencedaily.com/releases/2015/01/150121093507.htm.

38. M. Dworak and A. Wiater, "Media, Sleep and Memory in Children and Adolescents," *Sleep Disorders & Therapy* 2 (2013).

39. National Sleep Foundation, *2014 Sleep in America Poll: Sleep in the Modern Family, Summary of Findings,* 2014.

40. Drowsy Driving.org, "Facts and Stats," National Sleep Foundation, 2015.

41. National Sleep Foundation, *2014 Sleep in America Poll.*

42. M. Hysing et al., "Sleep and Use of Electronic Devices in Adolescence: Results from a Large Population Based Study," *BMJ Open* 5 (2015).

43. Dworak and Wiater, "Media, Sleep and Memory in Children and Adolescents."

44. Sakari et al., "Adolescents' Electronic Media Use at Night, Sleep Disturbance, and Depressive Symptoms in the Smartphone Age."

45. National Sleep Foundation, *2014 Sleep in America Poll.*

Chapter 4

1. G.S. Small et al., "Your Brain on Google: Patterns of Cerebral Activation During Internet Searching," *The American Journal of Geriatric Psychiatry* 17 (2009): 116–26.

2. K.L. Mills, "Effects of Internet Use on the Adolescent Brain: Despite Popular Claims, Experimental Evidence Remains Scarce," *Trends in Cognitive Sciences* 18 (August 2014).

3. J.N. Giedd, "The Digital Revolution and Adolescent Brain Evolution," *Journal of Adolescent Health* 51 (2012): 101–5.

4. J.Q. Anderson and L. Rainie, *Millennials Will Benefit and Suffer due to Their Hyperconnected Lives*, Pew Internet and American Life Project (Pew Research Center, 2012).

5. Mills, "Effects of Internet Use on the Adolescent Brain."

6. F. Tong and M.S. Pratte, "Decoding the Patterns of Human Brain Activity," *Annual Review of Psychology* 63 (2012).

7. L. Cattaneo and G. Rizzolatti, "The Mirror Neuron System," *Neurological Review* 66 (2009).

8. M. Iacoboni, "Imitation, Empathy and Mirror Neurons," *Annual Review of Psychology*, 2009.

9. M.D. Lieberman, *Social: Why Our Brains Are Wired to Connect* (New York: Broadway Books, 2014).

10. N.I. Eisenberger, M.D. Lieberman, and K.D. Williams, "Does Rejection Hurt? An fMRI Study of Social Exclusion," *Science* 302 (2003).

11. Lieberman, *Social: Why Our Brains Are Wired to Connect.*

12. Small et al., "Your Brain on Google: Patterns of Cerebral Activation During Internet Searching."

13. S.J. Blakemore, "The Developing Social Brain: Implications for Education," *Neuron* 65 (2010): 744–47.

14. J.N. Giedd, "Brain Development During Childhood and Adolescence: A Longitudinal MRI Study," *Nature Neuroscience* 2 (1999).

15. M.H. Johnson, "State of the Art: How Babies' Brains Work," *Psychologist* 13 (2000).

16. T.T. Brown and T.L. Jernigan, "Brain Development during the Preschool Years," *Neuropsychology Review* 22 (2012).

17. Giedd, "Brain Development During Childhood and Adolescence: A Longitudinal MRI Study."

18. J.H. Pfeifer and S.J. Blakemore, "Adolescent Social Cognitive and Affective Neuroscience: Past, Present, and Future," *Oxford Journals*, (2012).

19. A. Galvan et al., "Earlier Development of the Accumbens Relative to Orbitofrontal Cortex Might Underlie Risk-Taking Behavior in Adolescents," *The Journal of Neuroscience* 26, no. 5 (2006): 6885–92.

20. E.E. Forbes et al., "Healthy Adolescents' Neural Response to Reward: Associations with Puberty, Affect, and Depressive Systems," *Journal American Academy Child Adolescent Psychiatry* 49 (2010).

21. D.J. Siegel, *Brainstorm: The Power and Purpose of the Teenage Brain* (Tarcher, 2014).

22. L. Steinberg, "Cognitive and Affective Development in Adolescence," *Trends in Cognitive Sciences* 9 (2005).

23. S.J. Blakemore and K.L. Mills, "Is Adolescence a Sensitive Period for Socio-Cultural Processing?," *Annual Review of Psychology* 65 (2014).

24. M. Gardner and L. Steinberg, "Risk-Taking Among Adolescents, Young Adults and Adults: The Role of Peer Influence," *Developmental Psychology*, (2005).

25. Blakemore and Mills, "Is Adolescence a Sensitive Period for Socio-Cultural Processing?"

26. J.H. Pfeifer and S.J. Blakemore, "Adolescent Social Cognitive and Affective Neuroscience: Past, Present, and Future," *Oxford Journals*, (2012).

27. Siegel, *Brainstorm: The Power and Purpose of the Teenage Brain*.

28. D. Meshi, C. Morawetz, and H.R. Heekeren, "Nucleus Accumbens Response to Gains in Reputation for the Self Relative to Gains for Others Predicts Social Media Use," *Frontiers in Human Neuroscience* 7 (2013).

29. D.I. Tamir and J.P. Mitchell, "Disclosing Information About the Self Is Intrinsically Rewarding," *Proceedings of the National Academy of Science* 109 (2012).

30. A.D. Gindrat et al., "Use-Dependent Cortical Processing from Finger-Tips in Touchscreen Phone Users," *Current Biology*, (2014).

31. Lauren Sherman, *Dissertation Launchpad,* YouTube video, 2015, https://www.youtube.com/watch?v=bQ6owMqy-ZI&index=2&list=PLzuXAck6Rr0OzE6gz_uOicWz1pPrUJoNx.

32. Sookeun Byun et al., "Internet Addiction: Metasynthesis of 1996-2006 Quantitative Research," *Cyberpsychology and Behavior* 12, no. 2 (2009): 203–7.

33. A. Jaffe and Y. T. Uhls, "Internet Addiction—Epidemic or Fad?" *Psychology Today*, 2011, https://www.psychologytoday.com/blog/all-about-addiction/201111/internet-addiction-epidemic-or-fad.

34. D. Bavelier, C.S. Green, and M. W.G. Dye, "Children, Wired: For Better and for Worse," *Neuron* 67 (2010): 692–701.

35. S.J. Kirsch and J.R. Mounts, "Violent Video Game Play Impacts Facial Emotion Recognition," *Aggressive Behavior* 33 (2007): 353–58.
36. Giedd, "The Digital Revolution and Adolescent Brain Evolution."

Chapter 5

1. A. Lenhart et al., *Teens, Social Media & Technology Overview 2015*, Pew Internet and American Life Project (Pew Research Center, 2015).
2. R.F. Baumeister, "The Need to Belong: Desire for Interpersonal Attachments as a Fundamental Human Motivation," *Psychological Bulletin* 117 (1995): 497–529.
3. A. Nadkarni and S.G. Hofmann, "Why Do People Use Facebook?," *Personality and Individual Differences* 52 (2012): 243–49.
4. G.M. Chen, "Tweet This: A Uses and Gratifications Perspective on How Active Twitter Use Gratifies a Need to Connect with Others," *Computers in Human Behavior* 27 (2011).
5. R. I. Dunbar, A. Marriot, and N. D. C. Duncan, "Human Conversational Behavior," *Human Nature* 8, no. 3 (1997): 231–46.
6. Adrian Ward, "The Neuroscience of Everybody's Favorite Topic," *Scientific American*, July 16, 2013, http://www.scientificamerican.com/article/the-neuroscience-of-everybody-favorite-topic-themselves/.
7. M. Naaman, J. Boase, and C.H. Lai, "Is It Really about Me? Message Content in Social Awareness Streams," (2010).
8. Tamir and Mitchell, "Disclosing Information About the Self Is Intrinsically Rewarding."
9. T. M Brinthapupt and R.P. Lipka, "Understanding Early Adolescent Self and Identity: An Introduction," in *Understanding Early Adolescent Self and Identity: Applications and Interventions*, SUNY Series, Studying the Self (New York: State University of New York Press, 2002).
10. Ibid.
11. B.H. Clarke, "Early Adolescents' Use of Social Networking Sites to Maintain Friendship and Explore Identity: Implications for Policy," *Policy and the Internet* 1 (2009): 55–89.
12. K. Subrahmanyam and D. Smahel, *Digital Youth: The Role of Media in Development*. (New York: Springer, 2010).
13. d. boyd, *It's Complicated: The Social Lives of Networked Teens* (New Haven: Yale University Press, 2014).
14. Common Sense Media, *Social Media, Social Life: How Teens View Their Digital Lives*.

15. JWT Intelligence, "Gen Z: Digital in Their DNA," April 2012, http://www.jwtintelligence.com/wpcontent/uploads/2012/04/F_INTERNAL_Gen_Z_0418122.pdf

16. FTC, "Protecting Your Child's Privacy Online," 2013, http://www.consumer.ftc.gov/articles/0031-protecting-your-childs-privacy-online.

17. Y.T. Uhls, E. Zgourou, and P.M. Greenfield, "21st Century Media, Fame, and Other Future Aspirations: A National Survey of 9-15 Year Olds," *Cyberpsychology.eu*, (2014).

18. "FiveMillionFacebookUsersAre10orYounger," *ConsumerReports*,May10,2011, http://www.consumerreports.org/cro/news/2011/05/five-million-facebook-users-are-10-or-younger/index.htm.

19. Lenhart et al., *Teens, Social Media & Technology Overview 2015*.

20. M. Madden et al., *Teens, Social Media, and Privacy*, Pew Internet and American Life Project (Washington, DC: Pew Research Center, 2013).

21. "Teens Online," *Education.com*, February 18, 2011, http://www.education.com/reference/article/Ref_Teens_Online/.

22. Madden et al., *Teens, Social Media, and Privacy*.

23. H.A. Schwartz et al., "Personality, Gender, and Age in the Language of Social Media: The Open-Vocabulary Approach," *PLOS One* 8 (2013).

24. B.Gallagher,"No,SnapchatIsn'tAboutSexting,SaysCo-FounderEvanSpiegel," *Techcrunch*, May 12, 2012, http://techcrunch.com/2012/05/12/snapchat-not-sexting/.

25. Evan Spiegel, Keynote at AXS Partner Summit, January 25, 2014, http://www.scribd.com/doc/202195145/2014-AXS-Partner-Summit-Keynote.

26. A. Watts, "A Teenager's View on Social Media," 2015, https://medium.com/backchannel/a-teenagers-view-on-social-media-1df945c09ac6.

27. Lenhart et al., *Teens, Social Media & Technology Overview 2015*.

28. Ibid.

29. Watts, "A Teenager's View on Social Media."

30. Lenhart et al., *Teens, Social Media & Technology Overview 2015*.

31. M. Ito et al., *Hanging Out, Messing Around, and Geeking Out: Kids Living and Learning with New Media*, 1st ed., John D. and Catherine T. MacArthur Foundation Series on Digital Media and Learning (Cambridge, MA: MIT Press, 2009).

32. Madden et al., *Teens, Social Media, and Privacy*.

33. Y.T. Uhls, "To Allow Facebook or Not to Allow Facebook, That Is the Question," *Huffington Post*, April 24, 2012, http://www.huffingtonpost.com/yalda-t-uhls/facebook_b_1447506.html.

34. McAfee, "Cyberbullying Triples According to New McAfee 2014 Teens and the Screen Study," June 3, 2014, http://www.mcafee.com/us/about/news/2014/q2/20140603-01.aspx.

35. S.M. Coyne et al., "A Friend Request from Dear Old Dad: Associations between Parent–Child Social Networking and Adolescent Outcomes," *Cyberpsychology, Behavior and Social Networking* X (2013).

36. Kaplan Test Prep, "Kaplan Test Prep Survey: Percentage of College Admissions Officers Who Visit Applicants' Social Networking Pages Continues to Grow -but Most Students Shrug," 2014, http://press.kaptest.com/press -releases/kaplan-test-prep-survey-percentage-of-college-admissions -officers-who-visit-applicants-social-networking-pages-continues-to-grow -but-most-students-shrug.

37. CareerBuilder, "Number of Employers Passing on Applicants Due to Social Media Posts Continues to Rise, According to New CareerBuilder Survey," June 26, 2014, http://www.careerbuilder.com/share/aboutus/pressreleases detail.aspx?sd=6%2f26%2f2014&id=pr829&ed=12%2f31%2f2014.

38. "Asians in the Library," 2011, https://www.youtube.com/watch?v =zQR01qltgo8.

39. C. Gillam, "Missouri Mom Charged for Topless Hot Tub Photo with Teen Daughter," December 18, 2013, http://uk.reuters.com/article/2013/12/18/ us-usa-toplessmom-missouri-idUKBRE9BH1ID20131218.

40. Jon Ronson, "How One Stupid Tweet Blew Up Justine Sacco's Life," *NY Times*, February 12, 2015, http://www.nytimes.com/2015/02/15/magazine/ how-one-stupid-tweet-ruined-justine-saccos-life.html.

41. Careerbuilder.com, "Number of Employers Passing on Applicants Due to Social Media Posts Continues to Rise, According to New CareerBuilder Survey."

42. Steve Almasy, "Two Teens Found Guilty in Steubenville Rape Case," CNN, March 17, 2013, http://www.cnn.com/2013/03/17/justice/ohio -steubenville-case/.

Chapter 6

1. M.R. Leary and R.M. Kowalski, "Impression Management: A Literature Review and Two-Component Model," *Psychological Bulletin* 107 (1990): 34–37.

2. E. Goffman, *The Presentation of Self in Everyday Life* (New York: Anchor, 1959).

3. Alliance for Eating Disorders Awareness, "Eating Disorders Statistics," 2015, http://www.ndsu.edu/fileadmin/counseling/Eating_Disorder_Statistics.pdf.

4. B. Grosser, "What Do Metrics Want? How Quantification Prescribes Social Interaction on Facebook," *Computational Culture*, 2014, http://computational culture.net/article/what-do-metrics-want.

5. D.R. John, "Consumer Socialization of Children: A Retrospective Look at Twenty-Five Years of Research," *Journal of Consumer Research* 26 (1999): 183–213.

6. S. Harter, "Developmental Differences in the Nature of Self-Representations: Implications for the Understanding, Assessment, and Treatment of Maladaptive Behavior," *Cognitive Theory and Research* 14 (1990): 113–42.

7. Gardner and Steinberg, "Risk-Taking Among Adolescents, Young Adults and Adults: The Role of Peer Influence."

8. Erik Erikson, *Identity and the Life Cycle* (New York: International Universities Press, 1959).

9. D. Eder and S.K. Nenga, "Socialization in Adolescence," in *Handbook of Social Psychology*, ed. J. Delamater (New York: Kluwer Academic/ Plenum Publishers, 2003), 157–75.

10. J.E. Eccles et al., "Development during Adolescence: The Impact of Stage-Environment Fit on Young Adolescents' Experiences in Schools and in Families," *American Psychologist* 48 (1993): 90–101.

11. T.J. Dishion and J.M. Tipsord, "Peer Contagion in Child and Adolescent Social and Emotional Development," *Annual Review of Psychology* 62 (2011).

12. Meshi, Morawetz, and Heekeren, "Nucleus Accumbens Response to Gains in Reputation for the Self Relative to Gains for Others Predicts Social Media Use."

13. John, "Consumer Socialization of Children: A Retrospective Look at Twenty-Five Years of Research."

14. J. Anderson and L. Rainie, "Main Report: An In-Depth Look at Expert Responses,"n.d.,http://www.pewinternet.org/2014/05/14/main-report-an-in-depth-look-at-expert-responses/. (This comes from my own response to the survey.)

15. Y.T. Uhls and P.M. Greenfield, "The Rise of Fame: An Historical Content Analysis," *Cyberpsychology*, (2011).

16. D. Martin, "Child's Play," *Los Angeles Times*, November 22, 2009, http://articles.latimes.com/2009/nov/22/entertainment/la-ca-kids-celebrity22-2009nov22.

17. Y. T. Uhls and P.M. Greenfield, "The Value of Fame: Preadolescent Perceptions of Popular Media and Their Relationship to Future Aspirations," *Developmental Psychology*, (2012).

18. L. Kaufman, "Chasing Their Star, on YouTube," *New York Times*, February 1, 2014, http://www.nytimes.com/2014/02/02/business/chasing-their-star-on-youtube.html?_r=0.

19. K. Wallace, "Teen 'like' and 'FOMO' Anxiety," CNN, October 16, 2014, http://www.cnn.com/2014/10/16/living/teens-on-social-media-like-and-fomo-anxiety-digital-life/index.html.

20. V. Taylor, "Modern Teens More Worried About Missing Out Than Fitting In: Survey," *Daily News*, November 10, 2014, http://www.nydailynews.com/life-style/teens-worried-missing-fitting-survey-article-1.2005842.
21. James Franco, "The Meanings of the Selfie," *New York Times*, December 26, 2013.
22. D. Winneberger, "2013 AAFFPRS Membership Study," February 2014, http://www.aafprs.org/wp-content/themes/aafprs/pdf/AAFPRS-2014-Report.pdf.

Chapter 7

1. R.E. Bohn and J.E. Short, *How Much Information? 2009 Report on American Consumers* (San Diego: Global Information Industry Center, University of California, San Diego, 2009).
2. S.A. Brasel and J. Gips, "Media Multitasking Behavior: Concurrent Television and Computer Usage," *Cyberpsychology, Behavior and Social Networking* (2011).
3. "Google NGram Viewer," accessed April 13, 2015, http://books.google.com/ngrams.
4. Watts, "A Teenager's View on Social Media."
5. U.G. Foehr, "Media Multitasking Among American Youth: Prevalence, Predictors and Pairings" (Kaiser Family Foundation, 2006).
6. D.F. Roberts, U.G. Foehr, and V.J. Rideout, *Generation M: Media in the Lives of 8–18 Year-Olds* (Kaiser Family Foundation, March 2005).
7. Rideout, Foehr, and Roberts, *Generation M2: Media in the Lives of 8–18 Year-Olds.*
8. C. Wallis, *The Impacts of Media Multitasking on Children's Learning and Development* (Joan Ganz Cooney Center and Stanford University, 2010).
9. Foehr, "Media Multitasking Among American Youth: Prevalence, Predictors and Pairings."
10. C. Rosen, "The Myth of Multitasking," *The New Atlantis*, 2008.
11. P.E. Dux et al., "Isolation of a Central Bottleneck of Information Processing with Time-Resolved fMRU," *Neuron* 52 (2006).
12. E. Ophir, C. Nass, and A.D. Wagner, "Cognitive Control in Media Multitaskers," *Proceedings of the National Academy of Science* 106 (2009): 15583–87.
13. L. Lin, "Breadth-Biased Versus Focused Cognitive Control in Media Multitasking Behaviors," *Proceedings of the National Academy of Science* 106 (2009).
14. M. Minear et al., "Working Memory, Fluid Intelligence, and Impulsiveness in Heavy Media Multitaskers," *Psychological Bulletin Review* 20 (2013).
15. K. Subrahmanyam et al., "Learning from Paper, Learning from Screen: Impact of Screen Reading and Multitasking Conditions on Reading and

Writing among College Students," *International Journal Of Cyber Behavior, Psychology and Learning*, (2013).

16. Ibid.
17. M. Prensky, "Why YouTube Matters," *On the Horizon*, 2010.
18. D. Moore, "About Half of Americans Reading a Book," Gallup News Service, 2005, http://www.gallup.com/poll/16582/about-half-americans -reading-book.aspx.
19. K. Zickuhr and L. Rainie, *Younger Americans and Public Libraries*, Pew Research Center's Internet and American Life Project (Pew Research Center, 2014).
20. Rideout, Foehr, and Roberts, *Generation M2: Media in the Lives of 8–18 Year-Olds*.
21. L. Rutherford, M. Bittman, and J. Brown, "Effects of New and Old Media on Young Children's Language Acquisition, Development and Early Literacy: Findings from a Longitudinal Study of Australian Children," *Communication and Community: Proceedings of the 62nd Annual Conference of the International Communication Association*, 2012.
22. Subrahmanyam et al., "Learning from Paper, Learning from Screen: Impact of Screen Reading and Multitasking Conditions on Reading and Writing Among College Students."
23. Common Sense Media, "Zero to Eight: Children's Media Use in America."
24. J. Parish-Morris et al., "Once upon a Time: Parent-Child Dialogue and Storybook Reading in the Electronic Era," *Mind, Brain and Education* 7 (2013).
25. P.M. Mueller and D.M. Oppenheimer, "The Pen Is Mightier Than the Keyboard: Advantages of Longhand over Laptop Note Taking," *Psychological Science*, (2014).
26. Lenhart et al., *Teens, Social Media & Technology Overview 2015*.
27. B. Plester and C. Wood, "Exploring Relationships Between Traditional and New Media Literacies: British Preteen Texters at School," *Journal of Computer-Mediated Communication* 14 (2009).
28. B. Sparrow, J. Liu, and D.M. Wegner, "Google Effects on Memory: Cognitive Consequences of Having Information at Our Fingertips," *Science* 333 (2011).

Chapter 8

1. John Deasy, "Annual Address of LAUSD Superintendent to Adminstrators," Los Angeles, 2012.
2. Partnership for 21st Century Skills, *21st Century Student Outcomes* (Washington DC: Partnership for 21st Century Skills, 2009).

3. L. Cuban, *Oversold and Underused* (Cambridge, MA: Harvard University Press, 2001).

4. Jacquelyn Smith, "The Top Jobs for 2014," *Forbes*, December 12, 2013, http://www.forbes.com/sites/jacquelynsmith/2013/12/12/the-top-jobs-for-2014/.

5. M.Richtel, "InClassroomofFuture,StagnantScores," *New York Times,* September 3, 2011, http://www.nytimes.com/2011/09/04/technology/technology-in-schools-faces-questions-on-value.html?pagewanted=all&_r=0.

6. D.L. Silverall and MLTI Research and Evaluation Team, *A Middle School One-to-One Laptop Program: The Maine Experience* (University of Southern Maine: Maine Education Policy Research Institute, 2011).

7. "One Laptop Per Child Mission," Non-Profit, Laptop.org, 2015, http://one.laptop.org/about/mission.

8. J.P. Cristia et al., *Technology and Child Development: Evidence from the One Laptop per Child Program* (Institute for the Study of Labor, 2012).

9. Cuban, *Oversold and Underused*.

10. SRI International, *Blended Learning Report* (Michael and Susan Dell Foundation, May 2014).

11. B. McCoy, "Digital Distractions in the Classroom: Student Classroom Use of Digital Devices for Non-Class Related Purposes," *Digital Commons @ University of Nebraska–Lincoln* 71 (2013).

12. T. Karsenti and A. Fievez, *The iPad in Education: Uses, Benefits, and Challenges— A Survey of 6,057 Students and 302 Teachers in Quebec, Canada* (Montreal, Canada: CRIFPE, 2013).

13. Ibid.

14. D.E. Clayson and D.A. Haley, "An Introduction to Multitasking and Texting: Prevalence and Impact on Grades and GPA in a Marketing Class," *Journal of Marketing Education* (2012).

15. R.H. Kay and A. LeSage, "Examining the Benefits and Challenges of Using Audience Response Systems: A Review of the Literature," *Computers in Education* 53 (2009).

16. E. Kaasens-Noor, "Twitter as a Teaching Practice to Enhance Active and Informal Learning in Higher Education: The Case of Sustainable Tweets," *Active Learning in Higher Education* 13 (2012).

17. Clay Shirky, "Why I Just Asked My Students to Put Their Laptops Away," *Medium.com*, 2014, https://medium.com/@cshirky/why-i-just-asked-my-students-to-put-their-laptops-away-7f5f7c50f368.

18. S. Higgins, Z. Xiao, and M. Katsipataki, *The Impact of Digital Technology on Learning: A Summary for the Education Endowment Foundation* (Durham, England: Durham University, Education Endowment Foundation, 2012).

19. T.M. Philip and A. Garcia, "The Importance of Still Teaching the iGeneration: New Technologies and the Centrality of Pedagogy," *Harvard Educational Review* 83 (2013).

20. S. Jeong, H. Cho, and Y. Hwang, "Media Literacy Interventions: A Meta-Analytic Review," *Journal of Communications* 62 (2012).

21. Cuban, *Oversold and Underused*.

22. Silverall and MLTI Research and Evaluation Team, *A Middle School One-to-One Laptop Program: The Maine Experience*.

23. Philip and Garcia, "The Importance of Still Teaching the iGeneration: New Technologies and the Centrality of Pedagogy."

24. A. Melgosa and R. Scott, "School Internet Safety: More than 'Block It to Stop It,'" *Journal of Adventist Education*, (2013).

Chapter 9

1. *Jane McGonigal: Gaming Can Make a Better World*, Ted2010, 2010.

2. A. Lenhart et al., *Teens, Video Games and Civics*, Pew Internet and American Life Project (Pew Research Center, 2008).

3. Entertainment Software Association, *Essential Facts About the Computer and Video Game Industry*.

4. *Parenting in the Age of Digital Technology: A National Survey*.

5. K. Subrahmanyam and P.M. Greenfeld, "Effect of Video Game Practice on Spatial Skills in Girls and Boys," *Journal of Applied Developmental Psychology* 15 (1994): 13–32.

6. Y. Cheng and K.S. Mix, "Spatial Training Improves Children's Mathematics Ability," *Cognition and Development*, (2013).

7. D.H. Uttal et al., "The Malleability of Spatial Skills: A Meta-Analysis of Training Studies," *Psychological Bulletin*, (2013).

8. A. Eichenbaum, D. Bavelier, and C.S Green, "Video Games: Play That Can Do Some Serious Good," *American Journal of Play* 7 (2014): 50.

9. I. Granic, A. Lobel, and R.C.M Engeles, "The Benefits of Playing Video Games," *American Psychologist*, (2013).

10. M.W.G. Dye, C.S. Green, and D. Bavelier, "Increasing Speed of Processing with Action Video Games," *Current Directions in Psychological Science* 18 (2009): 321–26.

11. D. Giannotti et al., "Play to Become a Surgeon: Impact of Nintendo Wii Training on Laparoscopic Skills," *PLOS One* 8 (2013).

12. T. Stroback, P.A. Frensch, and T. Schubert, "Video Game Practice Optimizes Executive Control Skills in Dual-Task and Task Switching Paradigms," *Acta Psychologica* 140 (2012).

13. Cheryl Olson, "What the Tech," Rape Treatment Foundation, 2012.
14. W.D. Gunter and K. Daly, "Causal or Spurious: Using Propensity Score Matching to Detangle the Relationship Between Violent Video Games and Violent Behavior," *Computers in Human Behavior* 28 (2012).
15. M. Griffiths, "The Therapeutic Use of Videogames in Childhood and Adolescence," *Clinical Child Psychology and Psychiatry* 8 (2003).
16. Entertainment Software Association, *Essential Facts About the Computer and Video Game Industry.*
17. Ibid.
18. C.A. Anderson et al., "Violent Video Game Effects on Aggression, Empathy, and Pro-Social Behavior in Eastern and Western Countries: A Meta-Analytic Review," *Psychological Bulletin* 136 (2010): 151–73.
19. C.J. Ferguson and J. Kilburn, "The Public Health Risks of Media Violence: A Meta-Analytic Review," *The Journal of Pediatrics*, (2009), 759–63.
20. Gunter and Daly, "Causal or Spurious: Using Propensity Score Matching to Detangle the Relationship Between Violent Video Games and Violent Behavior."
21. Comment on "Your Child's Brain on Technology: Video Games" at Greatschools.org, May 7, 2014, http://www.greatschools.org/technology/7936-child-brain-development-and-video-games.gs.
22. M.S. Terlecki and N.S. Newcombe, "How Important Is the Digital Divide? The Relation of Computer and Videogame Usage to Gender Differences in Mental Rotation Ability," *Sex Roles* 53 (2005).
23. Subrahmanyam and Greenfeld, "Effect of Video Game Practice on Spatial Skills in Girls and Boys."
24. Steve Henn, "What Happened to Women in Computer Science?," NPR, October 21, 2014, http://www.npr.org/blogs/money/2014/10/21/357629765/when-women-stopped-coding.
25. J. Feng, I. Spence, and J. Pratt, "Playing an Action Video Game Reduces Gender Differences in Spatial Cognition," *Psychological Science*, (2007).

Epilogue

1. AVG, "Digital Birth: Welcome to the Online World," *Business Wire*, October 6, 2010, http://www.businesswire.com/news/home/20101006006722/en/Digital-Birth-Online-World#.VOIwyrDF_9t.
2. *Consumer Reports*, "Facebook and Your Privacy," July 2012.
3. K.M. Cutler, "Stats: Facebook Made $9.51 in Ad Revenue Per User Last Year in the U.S. and Canada," *Techcrunch*, May 3, 2012, http://techcrunch.com/2012/05/03/stats-facebook-made-9-51-in-ad-revenue-per-user-last-year-in-the-u-s-and-canada/.

4. K. Tummarello, "Google's Cerf: Social Rules, Not Laws, Will Protect Privacy," *The Hill*, November 19, 2013, http://thehill.com/policy/technology/190810-googles-cerf-social-rules-not-laws-will-protect-privacy.

5. E. Segran, "The Truth About Teenagers, the Internet, and Privacy," *Fast Company*, November 2014, http://www.fastcompany.com/3037962/then-and-now/the-truth-about-teenagers-the-internet-and-privacy.

REFERENCES

"2014 Sleep in America Poll: Sleep in the Modern Family, Summary of Findings." 2014.

Almasy, Steve. "Two Teens Found Guilty in Steubenville Rape Case." *CNN*, March 17, 2013. http://www.cnn.com/2013/03/17/justice/ohio-steubenville-case/.

American Academy of Pediatrics. "Children, Adolescents, and the Media," policy statement. American Academy of Pediatrics, 2013.

Anderson, C.A., N. Ihori, B.J. Bushman, H.R. Rothstein, A. Shibuya, E.L. Swing, A. Sakamoto, and M. Saleem. "Violent Video Game Effects on Aggression, Empathy, and Pro-Social Behavior in Eastern and Western Countries: A Meta-Analytic Review." *Psychological Bulletin* 136 (2010): 151–73.

Anderson, J.Q., and L. Rainie. *Millenials Will Benefit and Suffer due to Their Hyperconnected Lives.* Pew Internet and American Life Project. Pew Research Center, 2012.

Anderson, J.Q., and L. Rainie. "Main Report: An In-Depth Look at Expert Responses," n.d. http://www.pewinternet.org/2014/05/14/main-report-an-in-depth-look-at-expert-responses/.

APA. *Report of the APA Task Force on the Sexualization of Girls.* APA, 2010.

"Asians in the Library," 2011. https://www.youtube.com/watch?v=zQR01qltgo8.

AVG. "Digital Birth: Welcome to the Online World." *Business Wire*, 2010. http://www.businesswire.com/news/home/20101006006722/en/Digital-Birth-Online-World#.VOIwyrDF_9t.

"Baby Thinks Magazine Is a Broken iPad," YouTube, 2012. https://www.youtube.com/watch?v=2vXyx_qG6mQ.

Bandura, A. D. Ross, and S. Ross. "Transmission of Aggression Through Imitation of Aggressive Models." *Journal of Abnormal and Social Psychology* 63 (1961).

Baumeister, R.F. "The Need to Belong: Desire for Interpersonal Attachments as a Fundamental Human Motivation." *Psychological Bulletin* 117 (1995): 497–529.

Bavelier, D., C.S. Green, and M. W. G. Dye. "Children, Wired: For Better and for Worse." *Neuron* 67 (2010): 692–701.

Blakemore, S.J. "How Does the Brain Deal with the Social World?" *Neuro Report* 14 (2003): 1–10.

————. "The Developing Social Brain: Implications for Education." *Neuron* 65 (2010): 744–47.

Blakemore, S.J., and K.L. Mills. "Is Adolescence a Sensitive Period for Socio Cultural Processing?" *Annual Review of Psychology* 65 (2014).

Bohn, R.E., and J.E. Short. *How Much Information? 2009 Report on American Consumers.* Global Information Industry Center: University of California, San Diego, 2009.

Bora, Kukil. "Mobile App Store Annual Downloads To Reach 102 Billion In 2013; IOS, Android Stores To Account For 90% Of Downloads By 2017," 2013. http://www.ibtimes.com/mobile-app-store-annual-downloads-reach-102 -billion-2013-ios-android-stores-account-90-downloads.

Borba, Michele. "Parents Too Plugged In? That's What Our Kids Say." *Pediatric Safety*, 2012. http://www.pediatricsafety.net/index.php?s=She%E2%80% 99s%20always%20on%20her%20blackberry.%20It%E2%80%99s%20 soooo%20annoying.

boyd, d. *It's Complicated: The Social Lives of Networked Teens.* New Haven: Yale University Press, 2014.

Brasel, S.A., and J. Gips. "Media Multitasking Behavior: Concurrent Television and Computer Usage." *Cyberpsychology, Behavior and Social Networking* 0 (2011).

Brinthapupt, T. M, and R.P. Lipka. "Understanding Early Adolescent Self and Identity: An Introduction." In *Understanding Early Adolescent Self and Identity*, n.d.

Broadband Technology Fact Sheet. Pew Research Center, 2014. http://www .pewinternet.org/fact-sheets/broadband-technology-fact-sheet/.

Brown, J.R., and J. Dunn. "Continuities in Emotion Understanding from Three to Six Years." *Child Development* 67 (1996): 789–802.

Brown, T.T., and T.L. Jernigan. "Brain Development During the Preschool Years." *Neuropsychology Review* 22 (2012).

Byun, Sookeun, Celestino Ruffini, Juline E. Mills, Alecia C. Douglas, Mamadou Niang, Svetlana Stephchenkova, Seul K. Lee, et al. "Internet Addiction: Metasynthesis of 1996–2006 Quantitative Research." *Cyberpsychology and Behavior* 12, no. 2 (2009): 203–7.

Careerbuilder.com. "Number of Employers Passing on Applicants Due to Social Media Posts Continues to Rise, According to New CareerBuilder Survey," 2014. http://www.careerbuilder.com/share/aboutus/pressreleasesdetail.aspx ?sd=6%2f26%2f2014&id=pr829&ed=12%2f31%2f2014.

Cattaneo, L., and G. Rizzolatti. "The Mirror Neuron System." *Neurological Review* 66 (2009).

Chen, G.M. "Tweet This: A Uses and Gratifications Perspective on How Active Twitter Use Gratifies a Need to Connect with Others." *Computers in Human Behavior* 27 (2011).

Cheng, Y., and K.S. Mix. "Spatial Training Improves Children's Mathematics Ability." *Cognition and Development*, 2013.

Cisco. *"Cisco Visual Networking Index: Global Mobile Data Traffic Forecast Update 2014–2019 White Paper,"* February 2015. http://www.cisco.com/c/en/us/solutions/collateral/service-provider/visual-networking-index-vni/white_paper_c11-520862.html.

Clarke, B.H. "Early Adolescents' Use of Social Networking Sites to Maintain Friendship and Explore Identity: Implications for Policy." *Policy and the Internet* 1 (2009): 55–89.

Clayson, D.E., and D.A. Haley. "An Introduction to Multitasking and Texting: Prevalence and Impact on Grades and GPA in a Marketing Class." *Journal of Marketing Education*, 2012.

"CNN/ORC Poll," 2012. http://i2.cdn.turner.com/cnn/2012/images/04/16/rel4b.pdf.

Common Sense Media. *Social Media, Social Life: How Teens View Their Digital Lives*. Common Sense Media, 2012.

———. "Zero to Eight: Children's Media Use in America," 2013. http://www.commonsensemedia.org/research/zero-to-eight-childrens-media-use-in-america-2013.

Consumer Reports. "Facebook and Your Privacy," July 2012.

———. "Five Million Facebook Users Are 10 or Younger," 2011. http://www.consumerreports.org/cro/news/2011/05/five-million-facebook-users-are-10-or-younger/index.htm.

Coyne, S.M., L.M. Padilla-Walker, R.D. Day, J. Harper, and L. Stockdale. "A Friend Request from Dear Old Dad: Associations between Parent- Child Social Networking and Adolescent Outcomes." *Cyberpsychology, Behavior and Social Networking* X (2013).

Cristia, J.P., P. Ibarrarn, S. Cueto, A. Santiago, and E. Severin. *Technology and Child Development: Evidence from the One Laption per Child Program*. Institute for the Study of Labor, 2012.

Cuban, L. *Oversold and Underused*. Cambridge, MA: Harvard University Press, 2001.

Cutler, K.M. "Stats: Facebook Made $9.51 in Ad Revenue Per User Last Year In The U.S. and Canada." *Techcrunch*, May 3, 2012. http://techcrunch.com/2012/05/03/stats-facebook-made-9-51-in-ad-revenue-per-user-last-year-in-the-u-s-and-canada/.

Davies, J.J., and D.A. Gentile. "Responses to Children's Media Use in Families with and without Siblings: A Family Development Perspective." *Family Relations* 61 (2012).

Deasy, John. "Annual Address of LAUSD Superinendent to Administrators." Los Angeles, 2012.

Dishion, T.J., and J.M. Tipsord. "Peer Contagion in Child and Adolescent Social and Emotional Development." *Annual Review of Psychology* 62 (2011).

Dissertation Launchpad 2015—Lauren Sherman. YouTube, 2015. https://www .youtube.com/watch?v=bQ6owMqy-ZI&index=2&list=PLzuXAck6Rr0 OzE6gz_uOicWz1pPrUJoNx.

Drowsy Driving.org. "Facts and Stats," 2015.

Duerager, A., and S. Livingstone. "How Can Parents Support Children's Internet Safety?" *EU Kids Online*, 2012. http://eprints.lse.ac.uk/42872/1/How%20 can%20parents%20support%20children's%20internet%20safety(lsero).pdf.

Dunbar, R. I., A. Marriot, and N.D.C. Duncan. "Human Conversational Behavior." *Human Nature* 8, no. 3 (1997): 231–46.

Dux, P.E., J. Ivanoff, C.L. Asplund, and R. Marois. "Isolation of a Central Bottleneck of Information Processing with Time-Resolved fMRU." *Neuron* 52 (2006).

Dworak, M., and A. Wiater. "Media, Sleep and Memory in Children and Adolescents." *Sleep Disorders & Therapy* 2 (2013).

Dye, M.W.G., C.S. Green, and D. Bavelier. "Increasing Speed of Processing with Action Video Games." *Current Directions in Psychological Science* 18 (2009): 321–26.

"Eating Disorders Statistics," 2015. http://www.ndsu.edu/fileadmin/counseling/ Eating_Disorder_Statistics.pdf.

Eccles, JE, C Midgley, A Wigfield, CM Buchanan, D Reuman, C Flanagan, and DM Iver. "Development During Adolescence: The Impact of Stage-Environment Fit on Young Adolescents' Experiences in Schools and in Families." *American Psychologist* 48 (1993): 90–101.

Eder, D., and S.K. Nenga. "Socialization in Adolescence." In *Handbook of Social Psychology*, edited by J. Delamater, 157–75. New York: Kluwer Academic/ Plenum Publishers, 2003.

Eichenbaum, A., D. Bavelier, and C.S. Green. "Video Games: Play That Can Do Some Serious Good." *American Journal of Play* 7 (2014): 50.

Eisenberger, N.I., M.D. Liberman, and K.D. Williams. "Does Rejection Hurt? An fMRI Study of Social Exclusion." *Science* 302 (2003).

Ellison, N.B., C. Steinfeld, and C. Lampe. "Connection Strategies: Social Capital Implications of Facebook-Enabled Communication Practices." *New Media & Society*, 2010, 1–20.

Entertainment Software Association. *Essential Facts About the Computer and Video Game Industry*, 2014.

Erdley, C.A., and S.R. and Asher. "A Social Goals Perspective on Children's Social Competence." *Journal of Emotional and Behavioral Disorders* 7, no. 156 (1999): 156–68.

Eriksen, Erik. *Identity and the Life Cycle.* New York: International Universities Press, 1959.

FBI. "Uniform Crime Report," 2014. http://www.fbi.gov/about-us/cjis/ucr/ucr-publications#Hate.

Feng, J., I. Spence, and J. Pratt. "Playing an Action Video Game Reduces Gender Differences in Spatial Cognition." *Psychological Science*, 2007.

Ferguson, C.J., and J. Kilburn. "The Public Health Risks of Media Violence: A Meta-Analytic Review." *The Journal of Pediatrics*, 2009, 759–63.

Firth, C.D., and U. Firth. "Mechanisms of Social Congnition." *Annual Review of Psychology* 63 (2012): 287–313.

Foehr, U.G. "Media Multitasking Among American Youth: Prevalence, Predictors and Pairings." Kaiser Family Foundation, 2006.

Forbes, E.E., N.D. Ryan, M.L. Phillips, S.B. Manuck, C.M. Worthman, D.L. Moyles, J.A. Tarr, S.R. Sciarrillo, and R.E. Dahl. "Healthy Adolescents' Neural Response to Reward: Associations with Puberty, Affect, and Depressive Systems." *Journal American Academy Child Adolescent Psychiatry* 49 (2010).

Franco, James. "The Meanings of the Selfie." *New York Times*, December 26, 2013.

FTC. "Protecting Your Child's Privacy Online," 2013. http://www.consumer.ftc.gov/articles/0031-protecting-your-childs-privacy-online.

Gallagher, B. "No, Snapchat Isn't About Sexting, Says Co-Founder Evan Spiegel." *Techcrunch*, 2012. http://techcrunch.com/2012/05/12/snapchat-not-sexting/.

Galvan, A., T.A. Hare, C.E. Parra, J. Penn, H. Voss, G. Glover, and B.J. Casey. "Earlier Development of the Accumbens Relative to Orbitofrontal Cortext Might Underlie Risk-Taking Behavior in Adolescents." *The Journal of Neuroscience* 26, no. 5 (2006): 6885–92.

Gardner, M., and L. Steinberg. "Risk-Taking Among Adolescents, Young Adults and Adults: The Role of Peer Influence." *Developmental Psychology*, 2005.

Gentzkow, M., and J.M. Shapiro. "Preschool Television Viewing and Adolescent Test Scores: Historical Evidene from the Coleman Study." *The Quarterly Journal of Economics*, 2008.

Giannotti, D., G. Patrizi, G. Di Rocco, A.R. Vestri, C.P. Semproni, S. Pontone, G. Palazzini, and A. Redler. "Play to Become a Surgeon: Impact of Nintendo Wii Training on Laparoscopic Skills." *PLOS One* 8 (2013).

Giedd, J.N. "Brain Development During Childhood and Adolescence: A Longitudinal MRI Study." *Nature Neuroscience* 2 (1999).

———. "The Digital Revolution and Adolescent Brain Evolution." *Journal of Adolescent Health* 51 (2012): 101–5.

Gillam, C. "Missouri Mom Charged for Topless Hot Tub Photo with Teen Daughter," December 18, 2013. http://uk.reuters.com/article/2013/12/18/us-usa-toplessmom-missouri-idUKBRE9BH1ID20131218.

Gindrat, A.D., M. Chytiris, M. Balerna, E.M. Rouiller, and A. Ghosh. "Use-Dependent Cortical Processing from Finger-Tips in Touchscreen Phone Users." *Current Biology*, 2014.

Goffman, E. *The Presentation of Self in Everyday Life.* New York: Anchor, 1959.

"Google NGram Viewer," n.d. http://books.google.com/ngrams.

Granic, I., A. Lobel, and R.C.M Engeles. "The Benefits of Playing Video Games." *American Psychologist*, 2013.

Griffiths, M. "The Therapeutic Use of Videogames in Childhood and Adolescence." *Clinical Child Psychology and Psychiatry* 8 (2003).

Grosser, B. "What Do Metrics Want? How Quantification Prescribes Social Interaction on Facebook." *Computational Culture*, 2014. http://computationalculture.net/article/what-do-metrics-want.

"Growing Wireless: Quick Facts," 2015. http://www.growingwireless.com/get-the-facts/quick-facts.

Guernsey, L. *Screentime: How Electronic Media — from Baby Videos to Educational Software—Affects Your Child.* Basic Books, 2011.

Gunter, W.D., and K Daly. "Causal or Spurious: Using Propensity Score Matching to Detangle the Relationship Between Violent Video Games and Violent Behavior." *Computers in Human Behavior* 28 (2012).

Harrison, M.A., and A.L. Gilmore. "U Txt WHEN? College Students' Social Contexts of Text Messaging." *The Social Science Journal* 49 (2012).

Harter, S. "Developmental Differences in the Nature of Self Representations: Implications for the Understanding, Assessment, and Treatment of Maladaptive Behavior." *Cognitive Theory and Research* 14 (1990): 113–42.

Havas Worldwide. "The New Dynamics of Family." 2015. http://www.slideshare.net/HavasWorldwide/the-new-dynamics-of-family.

Hayne, H., J. Herbert, and G. Simcock. "Imitation from Television by 24- and 30-Month-Olds." *Developmental Science* 6 (2003): 254–61.

Henn, Steve. "What Happened to Women in Computer Science?" NPR, n.d. http://www.npr.org/blogs/money/2014/10/21/357629765/when-women-stopped-coding.

Higgins, S., Z. Xiao, and M. Katsipataki. *The Impact of Digital Technology on Learning: A Summary for the Education Endowment Foundation.* Durham University: Education Endowment Foundation, 2012.

Highlights magazine. "The State of the Kid, 2014." https://cdn.highlights.com/hfc/highlights/state-of-the-kid/Highlights-SOTK14.pdf?_ga=1.157347514.1483083552.1403891518.

Hysing, M., S. Pallesen, K.M. Stormark, R. Jacobsen, A.J. Lundervold, and B. Siversten. "Sleep and Use of Electronic Devices in Adolescence: Results from a Large Population Based Study." *BMJ Open* 5 (2015).

Iacoboni, M. "Imitation, Empathy and Mirror Neurons." *Annual Review of Psychology*, 2009.

"Internet Growth Statistics." *Internet World Stats*, 2014. http://www.internetworldstats.com.

"Intrusive Monitoring of Internet Use by Parents Actually Leads Adolescents to Increase Their Risky Online Behavior." *Science Daily*, 2015. http://www.sciencedaily.com/releases/2015/01/150121093507.htm.

Ito, M., S. Baumer, M. Bittanti, d. boyd, R. Cody, B. Herr-Stephenson, H. Horst, et al. *Hanging Out, Messing Around, and Geeking Out: Kids Living and Learning with New Media*. 1st ed. The John D. and Catherine T. MacArthur Foundation Series on Digital Media and Learning. Cambridge, MA: MIT Press, 2009.

Izard, C., S. Fine, D. Schultz, A. Mostow, B. Ackerman, and E. Youngstrom. "Emotion Knowledge as a Predictor of Social Behavior and Academic Competence in Children at Risk." *Psychological Science* 12 (2001): 352.

Jaffe, A., and Y. T. Uhls. "Internet Addiction—Epidemic or Fad?" *Psychology Today*, 2011. https://www.psychologytoday.com/blog/all-about-addiction/201111/internet-addiction-epidemic-or-fad.

Jane McGonigal: Gaming Can Make a Better World. Ted2010, 2010.

Jeong, S., H. Cho, and Y. Hwang. "Media Literacy Interventions: A Meta-Analytic Review." *Journal of Communications* 62 (2012).

John, D.R. "Consumer Socialization of Children: A Retrospective Look at Twenty-Five Years of Research." *Journal of Consumer Research* 26 (1999): 183–213.

Johnson, M.H. "State of the Art: How Babies' Brains Work." *Psychologist* 13 (2000).

Johnston, L.D., P.M. O'Malley, J.G. Bachman, J.E. Schulenberg, and R.A. Miech. *Monitoring the Future: National Survey Results on Drug Use, 1975-2013*. University of Michigan: National Institute on Drug Abuse at the National Institute of Health, 2013.

JWT Intelligence. "Gen Z: Digital in Their DNA." April 2012.

Kaasens-Noor, E. "Twitter as a Teaching Practice to Enhance Active and Informal Learning in Higher Education: The Case of Sustainable Tweets." *Active Learning in Higher Education* 13 (2012).

Kaplan Test Prep. "Kaplan Test Prep Survey: Percentage of College Admissions Officers Who Visit Applicants' Social Networking Pages Continues to Grow - but Most Students Shrug," 2014. http://press.kaptest.com/press-releases/kaplan-test-prep-survey-percentage-of-college-admissions-officers-who-visit-applicants-social-networking-pages-continues-to-grow-but-most-students-shrug.

Karl Fisch, modified by Scott McLeod. *Did You Know: Best of Shift Happens*, 2010. https://www.youtube.com/watch?v=jp_oyHY5bug.

Karsenti, T., and A. Fievez. *The iPad in Education: Uses, Benefits, and Challenges - A Survey of 6,057 Students and 302 Teachers in Quebec, Canada*. Montreal, Canada: CRIFPE, 2013.

Kaufman, L. "Chasing Their Star, on YouTube." *New York Times*. February 1, 2014. http://www.nytimes.com/2014/02/02/business/chasing-their-star-on -youtube.html?_r=0.

Kay, R.H., and A. LeSage. "Examining the Benefits and Challenges of Using Audience Reponse Systems: A Review of Teh Literature." *Computers in Education* 53 (2009).

Kirsch, S.J., and J.R. Mounts. "Violent Video Game Play Impacts Facial Emotion Recognition." *Aggressive Behavior* 33 (2007): 353–58.

Knapp, M.L., and J.A. Hall. *Nonverbal Communication in Human Interaction*. Seventh. Boston, MA: Wadsworth Cengage Learning, 2010.

Kuhl, P.K., F.M. Tsao, and H.M. Liu. "Foreign-Language Experience in Infancy: Effects of Short-Term Exposure and Social Interaction Onf Phonetic Learning." *Proceedings of the National Academy of Science* 100 (2003): 9096–9101.

Lauricella, A.R., T.A. Pempek, R. Barr, and S.L. Calvert. "Contingent Computer Interactions for Young Children's Object Retrieval Success." *Journal of Applied Developmental Psychology* 31 (2010): 362–69.

Leary, M.R., and R.M. Kowalski. "Impression Management: A Literature Review and Two-Component Model." *Psychological Bulletin* 107 (1990): 34–37.

Lenhart, A., M. Duggan, A. Perrin, R. Stepler, L. Rainie, and K. Parker. *Teens, Social Media & Technology Overview 2015*. Pew Internet and American Life Project. Pew Research Center, 2015.

Lenhart, A., J. Kahne, E. Middaugh, A. MacGill, C. Evans, and J. Vitak. *Teens, Video Games and Civics*. Pew Internet and American Life Project. Pew Research Center, 2008.

Lieberman, M.D. *Social: Why Our Brains Are Wired to Connect*. Broadway Books, 2014.

Limer, E. "The First Text Message Was Sent 20 Years Ago Today." *Gizmodo*, 2012. http://gizmodo.com/5965121/the-first-text-message-was-sent-20-years -ago-today.

Lin, L. "Breadth-Biased Versus Focused Cognitive Control in Media Multitasking Behaviors." *Proceedings of the National Academy of Science* 106 (2009).

Madden, M., A. Lenhart, S. Cortesi, U. Gasser, M. Duggan, A. Smith, and M. Beaton. *Teens, Social Media, and Privacy*. Pew Internet and American Life Project. Washington DC: Pew Research Center, 2013.

Madden, M., A. Lenhart, M. Duggan, S. Cortesi, and U. Gasser. *Teens and Technology 2013*. Pew Internet and American Life Project. Washington, DC: Pew Research Center, 2013.

Magill-Evans, J., C. Koning, A. Cameron-Sadava, and K. Manyk. "The Child and Adolescent Social Perception Measure." *Journal of Nonverbal Behavior* 19 (1995): 151.

Magill-Evans, J., K. Manyk, and A. Cameron-Sadava. "Child and Adolescent Social Perception Measure: Manual." Unpublished manuscript, 1995.

Martin, D. "Child's Play." *Los Angeles Times*, November 22, 2009. http:// articles.latimes.com/2009/nov/22/entertainment/la-ca-kids-celebrity 22-2009nov22.

Mazel, J. "The 50 Best Selling Videogames of the 1990s Worldwide," 2009. http://www.vgchartz.com/article/4145/the-50-best-selling-videogames -of-the-1990s-worldwide/.

McAfee. "Cyberbullying Triples According to New McAfee 2014 Teens and the Screen Study," 2014. http://www.mcafee.com/us/about/news/2014/ q2/20140603-01.aspx.

McCarthy, J. "Same-Sex Marriage Support Reaches New High at 55%." Gallup, May 2014. http://www.gallup.com/poll/169640/sex-marriage-support -reaches-new-high.aspx.

McCoy, B. "Digital Distractions in the Classroom: Student Classroom Use of Digital Devices for Non-Class Related Purposes." *DigitalCommons@University of Nebraska—Lincoln* 71 (2013).

Melgosa, A., and R. Scott. "School Internet Safety: More than 'Block It to Stop It.'" *Journal of Adventist Education*, 2013.

Meshi, D., C. Morawetz, and H.R. Heekeren. "Nucleus Accumbens Response to Gains in Reputation for the Self Relative to Gains for Others Predicts Social Media Use." *Frontiers in Human Neuroscience* 7 (2013).

Mills, K.L. "Effects of Internet Use on the Adolescent Brain: Despite Popular Claims, Experimental Evidence Remains Scarce." *Trends in Cognitive Sciences* 18 (August 2014).

Minear, M., F. Brasher, M. McCurdy, J. Lewis, and A. Younggren. "Working Memory, Fluid Intelligence, and Impulsiveness in Heavy Media Multitaskers." *Psychological Bulletin Review* 20 (2013).

Mlot, S. "Smartphone Adoption Rate Fastest in Tech History." *PC Magazine*, August 2012. http://www.pcmag.com/article2/0,2817,2408960,00.asp.

Moore, C., and P.J. Dunham, eds. *Joint Attention: Its Origins and Role in Development*. Erlbaum, 1995.

Moore, D. "About Half of Americans Reading a Book." *Gallup News Service*, 2005. http://www.gallup.com/poll/16582/about-half-americans-reading -book.aspx.

Mueller, P.M., and D.M. Oppenheimer. "The Pen Is Mightier Than the Keyboard: Advantages of Longhand over Laptop Note Taking." *Psychological Science,* 2014.

Naaman, M., J. Boase, and C.H. Lai. "Is It Really About Me? Message Content in Social Awareness Streams," 2010.

Nadkarni, A., and S.G. Hofmann. "Why Do People Use Facebook?" *Personality and Individual Differences* 52 (2012): 243–49.

Nowicki, Jr., S. "Manual for the Receptive Tests of the DANVA2," 2010.

NPD Group. "Internet Connected Devices Surpass Half a Billion in U.S. Homes, According to The NPD Group," 2013. https://www.npd.com/wps/portal/npd/us/news/press-releases/internet-connected-devices-surpass-half-a-billion-in-u-s-homes-according-to-the-npd-group/.

Olson, Cheryl. "What The Tech." Presented at the Rape Treatment Foundation, LA, 2012.

"One Laptop Per Child Mission." Non-Profit. Laptop.org, 2015. http://one.laptop.org/about/mission.

Ophir, E., C. Nass, and A.D. Wagner. "Cognitive Control in Media Multitaskers." *Proceedings of the National Academy of Science* 106 (2009): 15583–87.

Palsson, C. "That Smarts! Smartphones and Child Injuries." Department of Economics, Yale, 2014.

Parenting in the Age of Digital Technology: A National Survey. Northwestern University: Center on Media and Human Development, 2013.

Parish-Morris, J., N. Mahajan, K. Hirch-Pasek, R.M. Golinkoff, and M.F. Collins. "Once upon a Time: Parent-Child Dialogue and Storybook Reading in the Electronic Era." *Mind, Brain and Education* 7 (2013).

Partnership for 21st Century Skills. *21st Century Student Outcomes.* Washington DC, 2009.

Pascalis, O., M. de Haan, and C.A. Nelson. "Is Face Processing Species-Specific During the First Year of Life?" *Science* 296 (2002).

"Paul Ekman Group, Training," 2015. http://www.paulekman.com/products/.

Pfeifer, J.H., and S.J. Blakemore. "Adolescent Social Cognitive and Affective Neuroscience: Past, Present, and Future." *Oxford Journals,* 2012.

Philip, T.M., and A. Garcia. "The Importance of Still Teaching the iGeneration: New Techologies and the Centrality of Pedagogy." *Harvard Educational Review* 83 (2013).

Plester, B., and C. Wood. "Exploring Relationships Between Traditional and New Media Literacies: British Preteen Texters at School." *Journal of Computer-Mediated Communication* 14 (2009).

Plowman, L., and J. McPake. "Seven Myths About Young Children and Technology." *Childhood Education,* February 2013.

Prensky, M. "Digital Natives, Digital Immigrants." *On the Horizon* 9, no. 1 (2001): 1–6.

———. "Why You Tube Matters." *On the Horizon*, 2010.

Quinn, D., L. Chen, and M. Mulvenna. "Does Age Make a Difference in the Behavior of Online Social Network Users?" *IEEE International Conferences on Internet of Things, and Cyber, Political and Social Computing*, 2011.

Radesky, J., C.J. Kistin, B. Zuckerman, K. Nitzberg, J. Gross, M. Kaplan-Sanoff, M. Augustyn, and M. Silverstein. "Patterns of Mobile Device Use by Caregivers and Children During Meals in Fast Food Restaurants." *Pediatrics* (2014).

Radesky, J., A.L. Miller, K.L. Rosenblum, D. Appugliese, and J.C. Kaciroti. "Maternal Mobile Device Use During a Structured Parent–Child Interaction Task." *Academic Pediatrics* (2014).

Richtel, M. "In Classroom of Future, Stagnant Scores," *New York Times*, September 3, 2011. http://www.nytimes.com/2011/09/04/technology/technology-in -schools-faces-questions-on-value.html?pagewanted=all&_r=0.

Rideout, V.J., U.G. Foehr, and D.F. Roberts. *Generation M2: Media in the Lives of 8-18 Year-Olds*. Menlo Park, CA: Kaiser Family Foundation, 2010.

Robb, M.B., R.A. Richert, and E. Wartella. "Just a Talking Book? Word Learning from Watching Baby Videos." *British Journal of Developmental Psychology* 27 (2009): 27–45.

Roberts, D.F., U.G. Foehr, and V.J. Rideout. *Generation M: Media in the Lives of 8-18 Year-Olds*. Kaiser Family Foundation, March 2005.

Ronson, Jon. "How One Stupid Tweet Blew Up Justine Sacco's Life." *New York Times*, February 12, 2015. http://www.nytimes.com/2015/02/15/ magazine/how-one-stupid-tweet-ruined-justine-saccos-life.html.

Roseberry, S., K. Hirch-Pasek, and R.M. Golinkoff. "Skype Me! Socially Contingent Interactions Help Toddlers Learn Language." *Child Development* 85 (2014).

Roseberry, S., K. Hirch-Pasek, J. Parish-Morris, and R.M. Golinkoff. "Live Action: Can Young Children Learn Verbs from Video?" *Child Development* 80 (2009).

Rosen, C. "The Myth of Multitasking." *The New Atlantis*, 2008.

Rutherford, L., M. Bittman, and J. Brown. "Effec of New and Old Media on Young Children's Language Acquisition, Development and Early Literacy: Findings from a Longitudinal Study of Australian Children." *Communication and Community: Proceedings of the 62nd Annual Conference of the International Communication Association*, 2012.

Sabina, C., J. Wolak, and D. Finkelhor. "The Nature and Dynamics of Internet Pornography Exposure for Youth." *Cyberpsychology and Behavior* 11 (2008).

Sakari, L., N. Perkinson-Gloor, S. Brand, J.F. Dewald-Kaufman, and A. Grob. "Adolescents' Electronic Media Use at Night, Sleep Disturbance, and Depressive Symptoms in the Smartphone Age." *Journal of Youth and Adolescence* 44 (2014).

Schmidt, M.E., M. Rich, S.L. Rifas-Shiman, E. Oken, and E.M. Taveras. "Television Viewing in Infancy and Child Cognition at 3 Years of Age in a US Cohort." *Pediatrics* 123 (2009).

Schmidt, M.E., and E.A. Vandewater. "Media and Attention, Cognition and School Achievement." In *Children and Electronic Media*, 18:77. Future of Children 1. Princeton, NJ: Brookings Institute, 2008.

Schwartz, H.A., J.C. Eichstaedt, M.L. Kern, L. Dziuezynski, S.M. Ramones, M. Agrawal, A. Shah, et al. "Personality, Gender, and Age in the Language of Social Media: The Open-Vocabulary Approach." *PLOS One* 8 (2013).

Segran, E. "The Truth About Teenagers, the Internet, and Privacy." *Fast Company*, November 2014. http://www.fastcompany.com/3037962/then-and -now/the-truth-about-teenagers-the-internet-and-privacy.

Shirky, Clay. "Why I Just Asked My Students To Put Their Laptops Away." Medium.com, 2014. https://medium.com/@cshirky/why-i-just-asked-my -students-to-put-their-laptops-away-7f5f7c50f368.

Siegel, D.J. *Brainstorm: The Power and Purpose of the Teenage Brain.* New York: Tarcher, 2014.

Silverall, D.L., and MLTI Research and Evaluation Team. *A Middle School One-to-One Laptop Program: The Maine Experience.* University of Southern Maine: Maine Education Policy Research Institue, 2011.

Small, G.S., T.D. Moody, P. Siddarth, and S.Y. Bookheimer. "Your Brain on Google: Patterns of Cerebral Activation During Internet Searching." *The American Journal of Geriatric Psychiatry* 17 (2009): 116–26.

Smith, Jacquelyn. "The Top Jobs for 2014." *Forbes*, December 12, 2013. http:// www.forbes.com/sites/jacquelynsmith/2013/12/12/the-top-jobs-for-2014/.

Sparrow, B., J. Liu, and D.M. Wegner. "Google Effects on Memory: Congitive Consequences of Having Information at Our Fingertips." *Science* 333 (2011).

Sproull, L., and S Kiesler. "Reducing Social Context Cues: Electronic Mail in Organizational Communication." *Management Science* 32, no. 11 (1988): 1492–1512.

SRI International. *Blended Learning Report.* Michael and Susan Dell Foundation, May 2014.

Steinberg, L. "Cognitive and Affective Development in Adolescence." *Trends in Cognitive Sciences* 9 (2005).

Steiner-Adair, C. *The Big Disconnect: Protecting Childhood and Family Relationships in the Digital Age.* New York: HarperCollins, 2013.

Stroback, T., P.A. Frensch, and T. Schubert. "Video Game Practice Optimizes Executive Control Skills in Dual-Task and Task Switching Paradigms." *Acta Psychologica* 140 (2012).

Strouse, G.A., and G.L. Troseth. "Supporting Toddlers' Transfer of Word Learning from Video." *Cognitive Development* 30 (2014).

Subrahmanyam, K., and P.M. Greenfeld. "Effect of Video Game Practice on Spatial Skills in Girls and Boys." *Journal of Applied Developmental Psychology* 15 (1994): 13–32.

Subrahmanyam, K., M. Michikyan, C. Clemmons, R. Carillo, Y. T. Uhls, and P.M. Greenfeld. "Learning from Paper, Learning from Screen: Impact of Screen Reading and Multitasking Conditions on Reading and Writing Among College Students." *International Journal of Cyber Behavior, Psychology and Learning*, 2013.

Subrahmanyam, K., and D. Smahel. *Digital Youth: The Role of Media in Development.* New York: Springer, 2010.

Tamir, D.I., and J.P. Mitchell. "Disclosing Information About the Self Is Intrinsically Rewarding." *Proceedings of the National Academy of Science* 109 (2012).

Taylor, V. "Modern Teens More Worried About Missing out than Fitting in: Survey." *New York Daily News*, 2014. http://www.nydailynews.com/life-style/teens-worried-missing-fitting-survey-article-1.2005842.

"Teens Online." *Education.com*, February 18, 2011. http://www.education.com/reference/article/Ref_Teens_Online/.

Terlecki, M.S., and N.S. Newcombe. "How Important Is the Digital Divide? The Relation of Computer and Videogame Usage to Gender Differences in Mental Rotation Ability." *Sex Roles* 53 (2005).

Thompson, K.M, and F. Yokata. "Violence, Sex and Profanity in Films: Correlation of Movie Ratings with Content." *Medscape General Medicuine* 6 (2004).

Tong, F., and M.S. Pratte. "Decoding the Patterns of Human Brain Activity." *Annual Review of Psychology* 63 (2012).

Trends in the Prevalence of Sexual Behaviors and HIV Testing, 1991-2013. CDC, 2014. http://www.cdc.gov/healthyyouth/yrbs/pdf/trends/us_sexual_trend_yrbs.pdf.

Troseth, G.L., and J.S. DeLoache. "The Medium Can Obscure the Message: Young Children's Understanding of Video." *Child* 69 (1998): 950–65.

Tummarello, K. "Google's Cerf: Social Rules, Not Laws, Will Protect Privacy." The Hill, November 19, 2013. http://thehill.com/policy/technology/190810-googles-cerf-social-rules-not-laws-will-protect-privacy.

Turk, G. *Look Up*, 2014. https://www.youtube.com/watch?v=Z7dLU6fk9QY.

Uhls, Y.T. "To Allow Facebook or Not to Allow Facebook, That Is the Question," 2012. http://www.huffingtonpost.com/yalda-t-uhls/facebook_b_1447506.html.

Uhls, YT. "What Happens When Kids Go Cold Turkey from Their Screens for 5 Days?," 2014. http://www.huffingtonpost.com/yalda-t-uhls/what-happens-when-kids-go-cold-turkey-from-their-screens-for-5-days_b_5700805.html.

Uhls, Y.T., and P.M. Greenfield. "The Rise of Fame: An Historical Content Analysis." *Cyberpsychology*, 2011.

Uhls, Y. T., and P.M. Greenfield. "The Value of Fame: Preadolescent Perceptions of Popular Media and Their Relationship to Future Aspirations." *Developmental Psychology*, 2012.

Uhls, Y.T., M. Michikyan, J. Morris, D. Garcia, G.S. Small, E. Zgourou, and P.M. Greenfeld. "Five Days at Outdoor Education Camp Without Screens Improves Preteen Skills with Nonverbal Emotion Cues." *Computers in Human Behavior*, 2014. doi:10.1016/j.chb.2014.05.036.

Uhls, Y. T., E. Zgourou, and P.M. Greenfield. "21st Century Media, Fame, and Other Future Aspirations: A National Survey of 9-15 Year Olds." *Cyberpsychology.eu*, Forthcoming.

Uttal, D.H., N.G. Meadow, E. Tipton, L.L. Hand, A.R. Alden, and W. Warren. "The Malleability of Spatial Skills: A Meta-Analysis of Training Studies." *Psychological Bulletin*, 2013.

Wallace, K. "Teen 'like' and 'FOMO' Anxiety." CNN, 2014. http://www.cnn.com/2014/10/16/living/teens-on-social-media-like-and-fomo-anxiety-digital-life/index.html.

Wallis, C. *The Impacts of Media Multitasking on Children's Learning and Development.* Joan Gan Cooney Center and Stanford University, 2010.

Ward, Adrian. "The Neuroscience of Everybody's Favorite Topic." *Scientific American*, July 16, 2013. http://www.scientificamerican.com/article/the-neuroscience-of-everybody-favorite-topic-themselves/.

Watson, J. *Behaviorism.* New Brunswick, NJ: The People's Institute Publishing Company, 1924.

Watts, A. "A Teenager's View on Social Media," 2015. https://medium.com/backchannel/a-teenagers-view-on-social-media-1df945c09ac6.

Weisskirch, R.S. "Parenting by Cell Phone: Parental Monitoring of Adolescents and Family Relations." *Journal of Youth Adolescence* 38 (2009).

Winneberger, D. "2013 AAFFPRS Membership Study," 2013. http://www.aafprs.org/wp-content/themes/aafprs/pdf/AAFPRS-2014-Report.pdf.

Youth Violence: National Statistics. CDC, 2013. http://www.cdc.gov/violenceprevention/youthviolence/stats_at-a_glance/vca_temp-trends.html.

Zickuhr, K., and L. Rainie. *Younger Americans and Public Libraries.* Pew Research Center's Internet and American Life Project. Pew Research Center, 2014.

Zimmerman, F.J., Dimitri A. Christakis, and AN Meltzoff. "Associations Between Media Viewing and Language Development in Children Under Age 2 Years." *The Journal of Pediatrics* 151 (2007).

INDEX

ACKNOWLEDGMENTS

Without the love and support of my generous, kind, and talented writer husband, Jim, I would never have accomplished the enormous task of writing this book while working a full-time job, publishing my research, and bringing up our extraordinary children, Chloe and Walker. Chloe and Walker, who inspired most of my research ideas, as well as the many personal anecdotes in this book, I am so grateful for your willingness to talk to me about your lives and the media in it.

Thank you to everyone at Bibliomotion for guiding me on this journey: my publishing team, Sue Ramin, who reached out just at the right time, and her colleagues Erika Heilman and Jill Friedlander, and the entire team at Bibliomotion. You guys are a class act with an entrepreneurial spirit.

Thank you to Jim Steyer and Linda Burch—your support of my doctoral work and writing, while I also worked for Common Sense Media, was generous and rare; I love the organization you founded and am so glad to help support your important work. Thank you also to my many other talented colleagues at Common Sense, all passionate advocates for kids: Amy Guggenheim-Shenkan, Lisa Cohen, Dwight Knell, Amber Whiteside, Ellen Pack, Seeta Pai, Jill Murphy, Betsy Bozdech, Sierra Filucci, Christine Tasto, Rhianwen Brenner, Sarah Bowman, Lisa Solomon, Dana Blum, Paula Berry, and Joanne Gold, along with many, many others. I wish I could name you all, but I have a word limit!

Many friends stepped up to help me hone the chapters and provided me with invaluable feedback; thank you to Megan Hall,

Carrie Coltman-Arthur, Kate Prudente, Donna Weiss, Melissa Standish, Jennifer Curran, Katherine Wong, Claudine Romero Prestine, Cathy Lanigan, and Nathalie Benoit. You guys were willing to read these extremely rough chapters and the book improved drastically thanks to your contributions!

Thank you to Patricia Greenfield and Kaveri Subrahmanyam, my colleagues and friends at CDMC, for giving feedback and advice whenever asked. Patricia for being a fantastic mentor and always having my back. To Stuart Wolpert for being an advocate for our research and helping us share it with the world. And thank you to all my colleagues and collaborators Adriana Manago, Kristen Gillespie, Lauren Sherman, Stephanie Reich, and David Smahel. Thank you also to my dissertation committee Jim Stigler, Eran Zaidel, and Barbara Laurence.

Thank you to my fellow authors for support, advice, and encouragement: Peggy Orenstein, Amanda Enyati, Sarah Granger, Laura Nicole-Diamond, Paula Lee, and Cara Natterson.

To Rob Weisbach, for providing sage advice and guidance early in the process. To Bruce Feiler, who kindly made my book feel very real when he mentioned it in the *New York Times*.

And finally, in no particular order, for being supporters as I have wound down this road from Hollywood executive to mom to academic, author, and media expert—thank you to Paul Almond, Sheri Domke, Patty Kerr, Reveta Bowers, Brad Zacuto, Ellyn Weisel, Kristine Belson, Megan Sheridan, Lisa Henson, Brian Henson, Laurence Steinberg, Michael Levine, Catherine Steiner-Adair, Cameron Brown, Kristine Shannon, Helen Levin, Lycia Carmody, Susanne Daniels, Beth Bryson, Willow Bay, Stefanie Huie, Fonda Snyder, Halle Stanford, Rick Mischel, Minard Hamilton, Carol Lloyd, Christine Whitaker, Scott Johnson, Jaana Juvonen, Anne Peplau, Thad Phillips, Laura Leonhardt, Aviva Rosenthal, Laiko Bahrs, Vidya Sundaram, Chandri Navarro, Louise Landry, Nicole Lucas-Haimes, Erin

Herron, Rachel Iverson, Ashley Kramer, Lynn London, Shannon Gaulding, Andrea Feldman, Larry Cuban, Eric Mathre, Peter Levine, Chris Lawson, Michelle Kydd-Lee, Dan Aloni, Josh Goldstein, Stephanie Robinson, Jennifer Lieberman, Helen Kinnear, Tom Williams, Kelly Williams, Julie Wirshken, Elizabeth Giovine, Allison Rudi, Irene Kaufman, and all the others (I know I am forgetting many, and please forgive me) who offered to help me along this new journey as an author.

Last but not least, thank you to Dr. Maryam Kia-Keating, John Tehranian, my mother and father Drs. Mina and Monty Bissell, and my brother Dr. Ahrash Bissell.

ABOUT THE AUTHOR

Yalda T. Uhls is an award-winning child psychologist, researcher, and leading expert in the way media affects children. She is an unequaled and balanced voice in helping parents and educators navigate the overwhelming landscape of opinions, research, facts, conversation, and misinformation surrounding the impact of media on children. She has dedicated her entire career to media, first as a storyteller at movie studios such as MGM and Sony, and currently as a research expert on kids and media. Dr. Uhls works with schools, nonprofits, and companies, and her understanding of the academic literature, along with her many years of senior management experience in the entertainment industry, allows her a unique and relevant perspective, steeped in an understanding of the business world. She is passionate about translating science into useful knowledge and takeaways for parents, organizations, and educators. Her position is based in fact, relevant to all those concerned with using media in realistic and positive ways to shape youth development. In addition to her consulting and other work, Dr. Uhls works with Common Sense Media, a national nonprofit, as their director of creative community partnerships, and does research with UCLA. Companies that have sought out her expertise include Google LA, Henson Pictures, Disney Channel, and Hewlett-Packard.

Dr. Uhls's research focuses on how older and newer media impact the social behavior of preadolescents. The studies frequently have national impact and have been featured in *Time* magazine, the *New York Times, USA Today,* and NPR as well as in many scholarly publications. Notable awards include UCLA's Psychology in Action Award, for excellence in communicating psychological research to audiences beyond academia, and the Society for Research in Child Development's Outstanding Doctoral Dissertation. Prior to her academic career, Dr. Uhls spent more than fifteen years as a senior entertainment executive and producer. She holds an MBA, and a PhD in developmental psychology, from UCLA. Most importantly, as a mom of two digital teens (a boy and a girl) she has hands-on experience dealing with these issues.